Baptists
Who Dared

Baptists Who Dared

Frank T. HOADLEY & Benjamin P. BROWNE

Illustrated by WILLIAM HAMILTON

Judson Press ® Valley Forge

BAPTISTS WHO DARED

Unless otherwise indicated, Bible quotations in this volume are from *The Holy Bible,* authorized King James version.

Library of Congress Cataloging in Publication Data
Hoadley, Frank T.
  Baptists who dared.

  Twelve of the stories are adapted from Tales of Baptist Daring by B. P. Browne.
  Bibliography: p.
  1. Baptist—Biography. I. Browne, Benjamin P., joint author. II. Title.
BX6493.H6   286'.092'2 [B]   79-21695
ISBN 0-8170-0855-1

The name JUDSON PRESS is registered as a trademark in the U.S. Patent Office.
Printed in the U.S.A. ⊕

FOREWORD

The many Baptists who dared are beyond counting. Their passion for religious freedom, for telling the story of Jesus as they individually interpret it, for insisting upon the witness of believers' baptism, for proclaiming the social implications of their faith—these and other enthusiasms have repeatedly brought them into conflict with the power structures. But they have not been intimidated; they have held to their witness.

This small book contains only a few of the stories, but enough to give present-day Baptists a flavor of their heritage. Twelve of the stories are adapted from the book *Tales of Baptist Daring,* written by my good friend the late Benjamin P. Browne some two decades ago to meet a similar need. I have selected from Ben's tales those which seemed most effectively to demonstrate courage, hardship, and great risk, and I have shortened these somewhat to allow for the addition of eight other stories which have special significance to me as they demonstrate the same qualities.

The stories are as accurate historically as Dr. Browne and I have been able to make them. The incidents are true. The names, places, and dates are correct to the best of our knowledge. However, we have occasionally taken the storyteller's liberty of inventing some bits of conversation and a few minor details which are true in spirit if not in letter. I hope we may be forgiven for this device which adds interest to the tales.

I am deeply grateful to Mrs. Browne for making it possible for me to include so much of the work of her late husband in this book.

5

Ben Browne himself was a Baptist who dared, and he might well have been included among those whose stories are told here. As pastor, executive minister, editor-in-chief of Baptist curriculum materials, college and seminary president, and as president of American Baptist Churches in the U.S.A., he championed a variety of causes in which he followed his conscience against the resistance of others. I believe, however, that he would not have wanted me to write more about him than these few words in a work in which his name appears as one of the authors.

I also greatly appreciate the help of my wife, Margaret Walker Hoadley, for many valuable suggestions and for typing the manuscript. I would like, too, to thank my pastor, the Reverend Chester T. Winters, for making available his copious notes on Chaplain David Jones.

Frank T. Hoadley

CONTENTS

1 **ROGER and MARY WILLIAMS**
Pioneers of Liberty   **9**

2 **JOHN CLARKE and OBADIAH HOLMES**
Whipped with Roses   **15**

3 **JOHN BUNYAN**
A Great Author in Prison   **19**

4 **ISAAC BACKUS**
Horseman of Liberty   **23**

5 **DAVID JONES**
Chaplain in George Washington's Army   **27**

6 **ANDREW BRYAN**
Minister Among the Slaves   **33**

7 **WILLIAM CAREY**
"Expect . . . Attempt Great Things for God"   **37**

8 **ANN and ADONIRAM JUDSON**
Pioneer American Missionaries   **43**

9 **JOHN MASON PECK**
Church Builder of the West   **49**

10 **WILLIAM KNIBB**
   Emancipator of Slaves   55

11 **LOTT CAREY**
   First Black Missionary to Africa   59

12 **JOHANN GERHARD ONCKEN**
   Pioneer German Baptist Pastor   63

13 **ELLEN WINSOR CUSHING**
   Educator with a World Vision   69

14 **JOHN E. CLOUGH**
   Friend of the Outcastes   75

15 **WALTER RAUSCHENBUSCH**
   Prophet of Social Justice   79

16 **JOHN FROST**
   A Crow Indian Who Broke His Vow   83

17 **HELEN BARRETT MONTGOMERY**
   Forerunner of Today's Woman   87

18 **JENNIE CLARE ADAMS**
   Poet Laureate of the Hopevale Martyrs   93

19 **THOMASINE ALLEN**
   Where the Need Was Greatest   99

20 **MARTIN LUTHER KING, JR.**
   Preacher with a Dream   105

BIBLIOGRAPHY   111

1

ROGER and MARY WILLIAMS

Pioneers of Liberty

Through loose-fitting windows the cold east wind from Boston harbor blew into the courtroom. A lean-faced magistrate stirred and loudly spoke his mind: "This Roger Williams!—With his heretical beliefs he is unsettling our colony. The Scriptures warn us to have no dealings with such a man. I will have no more of his false teaching about freedom and about paying the Indians a larger price for the land. We must have him arrested forthwith and banish him to England."

For a moment the First Magistrate sat alone, reflecting upon Williams and the challenge he had brought to the peace and security of the colony. Looking out the window in that year of 1635, he saw a very primitive Boston, a little log-cabin settlement planted on three hills as a clearing in a dark forest where Indians lived. In the center of town were a cow pasture and a pond where a chorus of frogs croaked all night. There were no carts, no automobiles, and no streets as we know them today—just muddy paths which had been made by the trampling of cows.

A few miles to the north through the woods was Salem, another cabin settlement, where lived Roger Williams, the preacher who had come from England seeking freedom from the requirements and restrictions of the official state religion, the man with the independent beliefs, the one who insisted that the first allegiance of the settlers was not to the magistrates but to Almighty God. This was the Roger Williams who had the effrontery to preach that each man was free to follow the dictates of his own conscience before God.

9

BAPTISTS WHO DARED

The First Magistrate arose from his seat and strode toward a red-faced sea captain sprawled on a wooden bench. "Captain Wainright," the magistrate shouted, "we want you to sail your ship out of Boston harbor late this afternoon. Slip quietly into anchorage at Salem harbor, just about dark. Then, you and two of your crew members are to go to the log house of Elder Roger Williams and place him under arrest. Here are the papers."

The captain saluted and left on his assigned mission. But when the men reached Salem, they found no trace of Williams. Pounding on the neighbors' doors and demanding information, they learned nothing, for the good people of Salem somehow could not seem to recall having seen Williams lately, nor could they produce a suggestion as to where he might have gone. Thus Williams escaped the trap that had been set for him.

But no persecution is more relentless than religious persecution. Although Williams had successfully dodged the order of banishment, it still hung over him. He must flee quickly in order to escape a forced return to England without his family, or even worse, death. It was midwinter, and yet there was no place of refuge except the wilderness, where perhaps he could find friends among the Indians. Frail in health and alone, but strong in purpose, he set out. The northeast wind drove the stinging snow and sleet into his face. He lowered his head, pulled his broad-brimmed hat over his brow, and tightened the black cloth cloak around his shivering body as he trudged alone through the deep snow of his forest exile.

He traveled only six miles that day because of winter's early darkness. Stopping to build a bed of fir branches in a sheltered place, he heard a footstep. Turning quickly, he saw the welcome face of a faithful friend from Salem who had followed him, determined to share his hardships and ease his loneliness.

With a little fire of sticks and some water from under the ice in a stream, the grateful Williams made herb tea to warm them from the terrible chill. As they broke bread together, he told his friend: "In my pack I have only a sundial to tell the time, a Bible to feed my soul, and a loaf of bread to feed my body. But I have brought other things that are not in my pack. I have a stout heart to endure persecution because of what I know to be God's truth. I praise God that I may suffer for Christ's sake and for the cause of liberty of conscience for all men."

In the morning, their limbs stiff from sleeping on the frozen ground, the two men plunged bravely on through the wintry wilderness. Williams's goal was to find the Narragansett Indian friends with whom he had had many dealings in the past and who regarded him as a just and honest man. He was not disappointed. Some friendly Narragansetts found him when by the third day he had penetrated about thirty miles into the forest, and they offered him a place of shelter against the storms and cold. But even better fortune was to reach him there. Shortly after his arrival among the Narragansetts, a small group of members from his Salem church caught up with him, bringing his wife Mary and their two children, one of them only a few months old.

Mary was the light of Roger's life, and the unusual story of their romance is one in which we see the hand of God at work. Back in England, Roger had fallen deeply in love with a girl named Jane, who lived with an aristocratic aunt named Lady Barrington. Jane returned Roger's love, but in keeping with the custom of that time it was necessary for Roger to secure Lady Barrington's permission if he were to marry her lovely niece. When he went to her, however, she flatly refused. Why should she let her niece marry this poor young minister who had no property and no visible prospects of gaining any? Absolutely not!

Though Roger would not have believed it then, losing Jane was one of the best things that happened to him. This refined young lady, reared in the grand manner of her aristocratic aunt, was not cut out to endure hardship. She could never have survived the rigors of frontier life in Massachusetts. Much less could she have accepted the grueling experiences of wintry exile in forests and among Indians.

But there was a girl who could and, as Roger rebounded from his deep disappointment over Jane, he discovered her. She was Mary Barnard, a maid who worked in Lady Barrington's household. She was a strong, capable person, one who could stand with Roger in all circumstances, one who could raise and guide their children in the face of many hardships, and who could understand the meaning of doing it all for the principle of religious freedom. Furthermore, she was devout, a wife who prayed with him. Without Mary's encouragement and loyalty Roger might not have been so brave as to stand up to the oppressive leaders of the Massachusetts colony and to

make his perilous trip into the snowy forest to escape arrest.

When Mary joined him, therefore, in his exile among the Narragansett Indians, it was a time for great celebration. In June of that exile year, 1636, Roger and Mary went on to the historic venture for which they are best remembered. With their companions they crossed the river in a canoe and pressed on to discover a spring of fresh water. This would be their new home. Standing upon a rock, Roger Williams named the place Providence in honor of the God to whom he gave thanks for their safe arrival. Roger could see the hand of Divine Providence in all that had happened—finding Mary, coming to the New World, standing against the Massachusetts oppressors, and surviving that terrible winter. Truly it was Providence who had brought Roger and Mary to this historic moment.

Soon others joined Roger and Mary in the new settlement, and a colony was established which became our present state of Rhode Island. The leaders drew up a compact governing themselves "only in civil things"—which meant that the government would not try to dictate the religious beliefs and organizations of the people. This principle took further shape in 1640 when the colonists introduced a great new idea to the new world by stating formally that liberty of conscience was to be the ruling principle of their colony.

Today, of course, freedom of religion is guaranteed in the United States Constitution, but it was Roger and Mary Williams and the other settlers of Providence who first declared it on our shores. And, appropriately today, one of the most conspicuous features of the skyline of the city of Providence is the tall, graceful white spire of the First Baptist Church, founded by Roger Williams. It is said to be the first Baptist church in America, and it is a fitting memorial for Roger and Mary, who dared to stand for their beliefs.

2

JOHN CLARKE
and OBADIAH HOLMES

Whipped with Roses

The new colony in Rhode Island attracted many who were as dedicated in their search for religious freedom as were Roger and Mary Williams. Two of these were John Clarke and Obadiah Holmes.

Clarke, a physician, six feet tall, had come to America to get away from the religious persecution taking place in England. So had Holmes, a sinewy-muscled glassmaker. Both, however, found much the same situation in Massachusetts, though here it was the Puritans instead of the Church of England who held the power. Those who would not worship in the prescribed manner were punished by whipping, exile, or even hanging.

From Boston young Clarke wrote: "A year in this hotbed of religious tyranny is enough for me. I cannot bear to see men in these uttermost parts of the earth not able to bear with others in matters of conscience and live peaceably together. With so much land before us, I for one will turn aside, shake the dust off my feet, and betake me to a new place. There I shall make a haven for all those who, like myself, are disgusted and sickened by the Puritan dictatorship. I shall make it a place where there will be full freedom of thought and religious conscience."

That "new place" had to be Rhode Island. Clarke started packing. Remembering the experience of Roger Williams, he did not wait for an official order of banishment but took off for Providence. There Roger Williams advised him to settle in a beautiful seaside location farther south. Clarke liked the idea, established his home there, and in 1644 organized a church in what is now known as Newport. There he kept open house for other refugees from Puritan persecution, and lovers of liberty joined his settlement in great numbers.

One of these was Obadiah Holmes, who shared Clarke's commitment to Baptist principles. They became great friends. Together Holmes and Clarke did a great deal to build up the church and community of Newport. As the village doctor, Clarke would sit up all night with a patient to wait out the crisis of a fever. He would walk miles through the deep forest to reach the cabin of a poor pioneer woman who was having a baby. Along with his medicine and healing he also took the Bible and prayer.

One hot July day in 1651 Clarke and Holmes decided to visit William Witter, an aged and blind Baptist in Lynn, Massachusetts, who needed encouragement. It was an eighty-mile walk. Accompanied by another Newport Baptist, John Crandall, they set out with their Bibles, knapsacks, and guns. Witter, of course, was overjoyed when the travelers arrived, and before long they were conducting a Baptist service in his home. Then the troubles began. Constables, determined to break up the meeting, came and arrested all three of the visitors and forced them to attend services at the Puritan Church. As their protest to the service, Holmes, Clarke, and Crandall enraged the constables by refusing to take off their hats in the meetinghouse, and Holmes made it worse by heckling the preacher. Obviously they had to be punished.

Dragged ten miles from Lynn to Boston, the three were imprisoned for ten days before being brought to trial. Crandall was released, but Holmes and Clarke were sentenced to pay fines or to be publicly "well whipped." They refused on principle to pay the fines. However, an unknown benefactor paid Clarke's fine and obtained his release.

Holmes, on the other hand, was kept in prison for more than thirty days. Sympathizers tried to pay his fine, but he stubbornly refused their offers. "I will not accept deliverance in such a way," he said. By prayer, he prepared himself for the ordeal of the lashing.

While they were stripping Holmes of his clothing at the whipping post, he said to the gathered crowd: "Now I find that God does not fail me, and therefore now I trust him forever." Then the official in

16

charge of the lashing, spitting on his hands, gave the prisoner thirty strokes with a three-corded whip—equal to ninety strokes in all. As a result of this terrible flogging, the flesh of Holmes's back was reduced to jelly. But for Holmes this ordeal was a spiritual experience of God's presence. What he said to his persecutors when the whipping was over and done is a gem of Baptist history. He wrote: "When he had loosed me from the post . . . having joyfulness in my heart . . . I told the magistrates, 'You have struck me with roses.'" For many days he could not sleep except on his knees and elbows, for his back and sides were too raw and sensitive for any part of his body to touch the bed.

Other Baptists were denied many of the rights of citizenship, and they were subject to arrest, fines, prison, and the whipping post. Even to befriend Holmes was to be arrested and fined. Two men who shook hands with him were arrested and fined for their act.

It is of such heroic stuff that our Baptist ancestors were made, and something of this love of freedom and this resistance to all forms of oppression and slavery has come down through the ages to others. It is interesting to note that Abraham Lincoln was a great-great-great-great grandson of Obadiah Holmes, and perhaps it is not too farfetched to suggest that there was a touch of old Obadiah in Lincoln. Certainly both Holmes in his way and Lincoln in his upheld the principles of liberty and justice for all.

3

JOHN BUNYAN

A Great Author in Prison

"Midnight tonight under the big elm tree on the Ouse River!" they whispered to each other on the village streets and in the doorways. "You be a watcher against the coming of the constables," one told another. "Stand by the meadow-gate beyond the woods and whistle low if you see informers or constables approaching."

This secret meeting in the dead of night may sound like a robbers' rendezvous, but it was not. It was the way Baptists in seventeenth-century England had to gather at secret "baptizing places," because only the Church of England could legally hold services of worship.

In 1663 a twenty-eight-year-old tinker (or tinsmith) by the name of John Bunyan was led into the river to be baptized. This was a great event, because only two or three years earlier he had been, in his own words, "the very ringleader" of the town's youth "in all manner of vice and ungodliness . . . belching out oaths like a madman." But now John Bunyan rose from the waters as a new man fully surrendered to Christ, a powerful witness to his Lord.

Some of the good church members of Bedford suggested to Bunyan that he ought to preach. He hesitated because he was only an uneducated tinsmith who peddled in the streets. But preach he did, and people listened. They risked arrest to hear him preach in the woods, in barns, in the open air, in secret in homes, even at midnight, anywhere that they could quickly gather and disperse before the constables could catch them. In later years, as many as three thousand people gathered in London to hear him preach. Unlike

many other preachers of his time, he was on fire for God." "I preached
what I did feel," he said, "what I did smartingly feel under which my
poor soul did groan and tremble." Bunyan electrified his hearers, for
he spoke with the earnestness of "one sent from the dead."

But persecution was inevitable. Upon arriving at a secret Baptist meeting in a farmhouse, Bunyan was startled by the anxiety of the
congregation. "A warrant is out for your arrest, Brother Bunyan,"
said the leader. "You will certainly be sent to prison. If you will let us
call off the meeting now, there will be time for you to escape before
the constables get here."

Bunyan walked out of the farmhouse for a few minutes, but soon
he was back, his blue eyes flashing. "By no means will I run away. I
will not stir, nor will I have the meeting dismissed. Our cause is right.
We need not to be ashamed of it. To preach God's Word is so good a
work that we shall be well rewarded if we suffer for it."

And, of course, the constables came and took him before the
magistrates. The indictment charged that he "hath devilishly and
pertinaciously abstained from coming to church, and was a common
upholder of unlawful meetings"—thus defining his crime as having
attended Baptist services instead of those provided by the Church of
England.

For this offense Bunyan spent a total of twelve years in the
Bedford County Prison amid the dirt, the vermin, and the stench of a
rat-infested dungeon. The greatest punishment of all, perhaps, was
his separation from his wife and children, particularly his blind
daughter. From prison he wrote: "This parting from my wife and
poor children hath been to me as the pulling of my flesh from my
bones . . . also because I should have often brought to my mind the
hardships, miseries, and wants my poor family was like to meet with
should I be taken from them, especially my poor blind child who lays
nearer to my heart than all else besides."

But he wrote much more than this from prison. The tinker
became the thinker. Books and pamphlets poured from his pen and
were read by thousands. He had a vivid imagination; he knew the
language of the people; and he was a genius with his pen.

Bunyan is remembered for one book in particular. After long
reflection and much practice in writing, toward the last part of his
prison confinement, he began to write a wonderful story, an allegory

so vibrant with interest, so sparkling with realism, and so spiritually refreshing, that his publishers had to print a second edition before the first year ended. More than one hundred thousand copies were sold in the seventeenth century, and untold thousands in more than a hundred languages have been sold since that time. You can still find it in a book store or borrow it from a library. It is one of the great classics of all time. Its title is *The Pilgrim's Progress.* It is alive with lions and giants, with castles and maidens, with judges and juries, with Vanity Fair, the Pope, and humorous and serious characters that make it great reading. Among his most picturesque characters are the fat and sleepy Mr. Worldly Wiseman, the willowy Mr. Pliable, and the unreliable Mr. Facing Both Ways.

Through his prison writings and particularly *The Pilgrim's Progress,* Bunyan continued his ministry even more effectively than by his preaching in earlier years. By the simplicity, directness, and vividness with which he wrote, Bunyan gave the gospel widespread appeal. At the same time he bore witness to the Baptist convictions which he held so firmly that he stayed in prison when he might have secured his release merely by attending the Church of England and refraining from Baptist preaching.

Finally, after twelve years he was released from his imprisonment, but our story does not end, for he went on writing other books that became religious classics, and some of them are still read. Thus his ministry spread across the world and down the centuries.

One last incident in his life shows Bunyan's dedication. While always an unyielding man of principle, he was also a peacemaker. A young neighbor in Bedford had incurred the wrath of his father, who lived in Reading. The father had decided to disinherit him, and the son asked Bunyan to seek a reconciliation. Bunyan was in no condition to travel. All that spring he had suffered severely from influenza. Yet, weak as he was, he rode horseback more than fifty miles, preached in a church that night, and next morning called on the father, persuading him to relent and send for his son.

Mission accomplished, he set off for London. On the way a cloudburst of rain blinded his horse, who frequently stumbled, and Bunyan became drenched. On arrival he was so weak that he could scarcely dismount from his horse. Quickly his friends gave him hot drinks and tucked him in bed to end his chill.

Feeling slightly better the next day, he sat up in bed and finished writing his last book, *The Acceptable Sacrifice*. Sick as he was, on Sunday he insisted on keeping his engagement to preach at Whitechapel meetinghouse. From the pulpit he returned to bed with a high fever. His once strong physique was now too much weakened by his long years in prison, his arduous labors, and his recent drenching ride to recover from the strain of his illness. And so he died.

Of all the persecuted Baptists, Bunyan was longest in prison. Alone among Baptists he produced a classic of literature still widely read and treasured after three centuries. Even today you might enjoy reading *The Pilgrim's Progress*. And perhaps you have sung his hymn which in brief form embodies the ideas of the book. It is titled "He Who Would Valiant Be." It is sung in churches of a great many denominations—including, interestingly enough, the Church of England.

4

ISAAC BACKUS

Horseman of Liberty

It was mid-August of 1724, and sixteen-year-old Isaac Backus was cutting hay on his father's farm. Beneath the blazing sun, with streams of sweat trickling down his bare chest and back, he swung his scythe in wide, sweeping arcs. Something was on his mind. As he slashed into a clump of daisies, they fell limply to the ground, and unexpectedly some words flashed into his mind: "Man is as the flower of the field. Today he flourisheth, tomorrow he is cut down and withereth." Suddenly he laid the scythe down and sat in the cool shade of a nearby oak. It was time to wrestle with his disturbing problem. He could not put it off any longer.

What was on his mind was indeed serious. A great revival of religion was sweeping across New England. An English preacher named George Whitefield had been eloquently calling people to Christ, and they had been responding in great numbers. Isaac too had been stirred. Suddenly, now, he felt himself to be a "hardened sinner" in need of the Savior. He fell on his knees and in earnest and heartfelt prayer surrendered himself to Christ.

Describing this event, he later wrote: "My soul yielded all into his hands, fell at his feet, and was silent and calm before him. . . . The Word of God and the promises of his grace appeared firmer than a rock, and I was astonished at my previous unbelief. My heavy burden was gone, tormenting fears were fled, and my joy was unspeakable."

But what to do about it? Sometime later, again on the edge of the woods, he meditated and prayed. This time there came to him a call to preach, a clear and powerful conviction that God wanted him for the

ministry. Though only twenty-two years old, Backus felt so certain of his new calling that he preached on the following Sunday. Those who heard him agreed that he was truly called by God to preach the gospel.

Soon he became the pastor of a Congregational church in Middleborough, Massachusetts. Studying the Bible intently as he prepared his sermons, he began to have questions in his mind about baptism, and in 1749 he began an intensive study to discover whether or not the Bible taught infant baptism. Finally, convinced that it did not, he led six members of the church into the water to be baptized, and they formed the Middleborough Baptist Church.

The weak, abused, and persecuted Baptists of New England now found in this young minister their stoutest champion. His convictions respecting the rights of conscience moved him to the forefront of the battle for freedom of religious faith, just at the time when the American colonists were beginning to speak of political liberty with the cry of "No taxation without representation!" The two causes were closely intertwined, because in much of New England all people were compelled to support the official church (originally known as Puritan, but now as Congregational), whether they attended it or not.

Backus had seen people arrested, imprisoned, and their property confiscated because they could not in good conscience pay taxes forced upon them to support a church in which they did not believe. His own mother, Elizabeth Backus, had been held in jail for two weeks because she would not support the established church. Later, he too had been imprisoned until a friend paid the fine which he himself had refused to pay. In Ashfield, Massachusetts, nearly four hundred acres of land belonging to the Baptists had been sold, and the money used as religious taxes, to help build a Congregational church.

In Pepperel, forty miles from Boston, a small company of Baptists met by the river to baptize six new converts. A mob gathered and baptized a dog in the river to ridicule them. When the believers moved their service to another river on the opposite side of town, the mob followed and baptized three more dogs. Feeling was now running so high that the town officials advised the Baptist ministers to leave town immediately for their own safety. Finally, in yet another location, they held the baptismal service with the mob still jeering.

BAPTISTS WHO DARED

Aroused by events like these, a group of Baptist churches combined their interests in what was called the Warren Association. They appointed Backus as their official agent to travel about and fight in behalf of religious liberty wherever the need might be. They chose well, for Backus became known as one of the most aggressive Yankees the colonies ever reared.

Carrying out his work, Backus rode horseback to present to the First Continental Congress in Philadelphia, on behalf of the Baptists, a petition for religious liberty. This required much courage. He was rebuffed by the committee of the Congress and attacked in the press. In one newspaper article he was threatened with "a halter and the gallows."

Failing in this presentation, he then drew up a memorial petition of the Baptist churches and presented it to the Provincial Congress in Cambridge, Massachusetts. Next, he presented a memorial petition to the Colonial Assembly in Watertown, Massachusetts. There was no mincing of words in these petitions. Backus was an able draftsman and was soon known as the champion of nonconformity in New England.

Though Backus was uneducated, his abilities as a preacher, defender of liberty, and writer were widely recognized. Various Baptist leaders urged him to write a history of the Baptist churches in New England, and he did—in three volumes totaling 1,300 pages, which are still highly regarded as an important source of early American history.

His fame and abilities spread far among Baptists, and churches in the South asked for his assistance. He spent six months in Virginia and North Carolina, traveling more than 3,000 miles on horseback and preaching at least 126 sermons. He served for 60 years as a minister of the gospel and died at the age of 83, a Baptist hero who belongs to all people who love liberty in every age.

5

DAVID JONES

Chaplain in George Washington's Army

The Reverend Dr. David Jones was arguing with his wife again. "Just who said a minister can't fight?" he demanded, scowling. "Just because those fuzzy-cheeked lads in the army can't preach doesn't mean that I can't *both* fight and preach. Why should I be penalized for having two talents?"

Ann stood and glared, her hands placed firmly upon her hips. "Well, Ann, what can I do?" he asked.

"You could use that one talent now and bide your time for the future," she said as she met his gaze.

"I want to fight now."

"There's no enemy to fight here at the moment, David, but there are quite a few friends who could use the confidence of the Bible about the fight that's coming."

David smiled. Yes, unquestionably there was a fight coming, if in fact it had not already begun. For more than ten years there had been trouble between the American colonists and the British who ruled them. The mother country had oppressed them with unfair and excessive taxes, burdensome trade restrictions, and the stationing of unwanted troops in New York and Boston. In retaliation the Americans had dumped a shipload of tea into Boston harbor, had called two Continental Congresses in Philadelphia to present their grievances to the English king, and had taken arms against the British soldiers at Lexington, Concord, and Bunker Hill. Even now the Second Continental Congress had chosen Thursday, July 20, 1775, as a special day of fasting and prayer when ministers were asked to preach to the troops and other citizens.

BAPTISTS WHO DARED

This special day was David Jones's great opportunity to exercise his preaching talent on behalf of his fellow Americans. As the new pastor of the Baptist Church in the Great Valley, twenty miles northwest of Philadelphia, he would have a ready congregation of farmers as well as the newly recruited regiment of Colonel Dewees to hear his sermon. He labored hard in preparation and finally produced his masterpiece. When the day arrived, the colonel's three hundred untrained soldiers were there, not very well uniformed or armed but standing at attention in the yard before the log meeting-house of the church and augmented by a large gathering of men, women, and children who sat on the grass or in their farm wagons.

Dr. Jones announced his text from Nehemiah 4:14, "Be not ye afraid of them: remember the Lord, which is great and terrible, and fight for your brethren, your sons, and your daughters, your wives, and your houses." As he neared the sermon's climax after some seven thousand eloquent words of argument and exhortation, he summarized his thoughts: "I hope that it has been made evident, that defensive war is sinless, and consistent with the purest religion. . . . Seeing, therefore, that it is sinless, and we are called to take the bloody weapons of death in hand, let not the expense of war discourage us. This indeed must be very great, but be it so; we fight not for present profit, no, our noble struggle is for liberty itself, without which even life would be miserable. . . . Let me therefore entreat you seriously to lay to heart the present state, and 'remember the Lord, which is great and terrible.'"

The enthusiastic response of his open-air congregation to these stirring words convinced Jones that he was right about wanting to enter the army. How could he urge others to face the hardships and dangers of war if he was not willing to do so himself? Within a few months he appeared before his congregation at the Great Valley church and announced that he was leaving to become a chaplain in the Continental Army—the second clergyman and the first Baptist in the history of America to so declare.* Tradition says that he did so by

---

* William Emerson, grandfather of the famous writer Ralph Waldo Emerson, was the first, having served at the Battle of Concord. Both of these were informal appointments. David Jones was also the second to become officially a chaplain in the United States Army—the *only* one at the time, replacing John Hurt, in 1790, who had recently resigned.

wearing a pulpit robe when he preached on that memorable Sunday and removing it at the close of the sermon to reveal his military uniform.

This intrepid, lanky preacher with long black hair and a long-beaked nose was no newcomer to adventure. Before settling in the Great Valley he had made two trips on horseback, more than three hundred miles each way, to minister to the Shawnee and Delaware Indians along the Ohio River. He was something of a showman, too, always dressing in the highly ornamented cocked hat, knee breeches, and buckled shoes of a colonial gentleman. When he spoke to the soldiers, he insisted on a roll of the drums to command their attention. He spoke very movingly; it was said that he could have an audience laughing at one moment and crying at the next.

During most of the Revolutionary War he was assigned to the First Pennsylvania Brigade under Colonel (later General) Anthony Wayne—known as "Mad Anthony" because of his reckless courage. There were few major events in the war that Jones missed; he was at Ticonderoga, Morristown, and Brandywine. He narrowly escaped being killed at the Paoli Massacre. He spent the miserable winter of 1777–78 with the troops at Valley Forge, just a couple of miles from the Great Valley church. He returned to Morristown for another severe and difficult winter. He traveled with the troops through long, tedious, indecisive campaigns in Pennsylvania, New Jersey, and New York. Finally, when victory came at Yorktown in 1781, he was present at the surrender of Lord Cornwallis. Through it all he preached to the soldiers urging them to be brave in spite of peril and hardships; he exhorted them to remain faithful to the moral teachings of their youth; he comforted them when wounded and conducted their funerals when they perished. In all these ways he helped to set the pattern for thousands of military chaplains who were to follow him in later years and centuries.

David Jones's idea of the chaplaincy, however, went beyond that which we find acceptable today. He was frankly a fighter. He would carry a pistol or a musket and was not unwilling to use it in battle. The story is told of one time when Chaplain Jones saw a horse tied outside a tavern near Valley Forge and suspected that its owner might be a British soldier. Going into the bar, he heard a voice inquiring for directions to the Germantown Road. Although the man was in civilian dress, Jones realized that only a British spy would be seeking this particular information at that time, and so at gunpoint he made the man his prisoner. It is said that the poor spy was so embarrassed over the ridicule which he received from his fellow Englishmen for having been captured by a chaplain that he became a deserter after having been returned to his own army in an exchange of prisoners.

Jones served the army as a medical man also. He had a respectable knowledge of medicine and surgery and was very helpful in treating the wounded. He learned to remove bullets by the crude and bloody methods then available and to amputate infected arms and legs of soldiers who had no anesthetic but a stiff drink of whiskey. Unlike the other medics, Jones included prayer among his collection of remedies and cures, and many times it worked.

He became notorious among the British. They put a price on his head, but they never succeeded in catching him. They worked their vengeance, however, against Jones's beloved Baptist Church in the Great Valley, which they plundered of all the valuables they could find, including its pewter Communion ware, pulpit Bible, baptismal garments, and cemetery tools.

When the Revolutionary War was over and American independence was secure, Jones returned to the pastoral ministry for a while. Then the call came again to serve under General Wayne in a military campaign, this time in frontier wars against the Indian tribes who had been incited by the British, whereupon he spent five more years as a chaplain and adviser to Wayne. When Wayne died in 1796, Jones returned to the pastorate of the Great Valley church. It was not until 1809 that he was able to preach a funeral sermon for his great leader, when Wayne's body was moved from its first grave near Erie, Pennsylvania, to St. David's Episcopal Church near the Great Valley.

The Reverend Dr. Jones was seventy-six years old when the War of 1812 broke out and once more America was in conflict with England. We might think this distinguished gentleman had had enough of military service by that time, but no! Once more he volunteered and was appointed chaplain in the Northern Department of the Army. An American officer on the Canadian frontier reports the arrival of Chaplain Jones: "When the venerable chaplain arrived at the lines, he held a religious service, and such was the patriotic fervor of the prayer with which it was concluded, that the troops spontaneously responded with three hearty cheers."

Dr. Jones lived another eight years after that. One of his last public addresses was delivered at the dedication of the monument commemorating the Paoli Massacre, where he had narrowly escaped death in one of the first experiences of his military career.

David Jones was the first great military chaplain of a long succession which continues to the present day. Since his time it has been made clear that a chaplain's duty is to bring spiritual counsel, comfort, and moral guidance to the troops, not to fight by their sides or to provide them with medical care, but this specified duty in itself is a great responsibility requiring bravery and commitment. Today's chaplain in the army, navy, or air force is a pastor to the people under whatever conditions circumstances may require, whether pleasant or absolutely terrifying. Many chaplains have acted with unbelievable heroism under fire, bringing spiritual help at great physical peril to themselves and sometimes sacrificing their own lives that others might survive. Some have displayed bravery of a different kind, challenging military customs and traditions and defying the establishment to bring needed reforms in the military way of life. Chaplains come in all sizes, shapes, colors, and flavors; they include most of the religious bodies found in the United States, and of course only a relatively small percentage come from any one denomination. Baptists are proud to claim not only David Jones, their first, but also the distinguished line of his successors.

6

ANDREW BRYAN

Minister Among the Slaves

To be a black person in America has never been easy, and it was especially hard in the late 1700s, when most black people were still slaves. Being a slave meant that you could scarcely claim to be a person; in the eyes of society and of the law, you were property. You could be bought and sold. Your owner, or master, might be kind and compassionate or he might be cruel and harsh, but in either circumstance he "kept you in your place"—that is, he dictated the hours and conditions of your work and even of your personal life. You could not leave his property, nor could you marry, worship, or study without his permission.

Schools and churches were particularly suspect. Most owners disapproved of their slaves going to school because it took valuable time away from their work and might expose them to ideas which would make them dissatisfied with their condition. Worship was acceptable if it kept the slaves contented and did not take too much time, but not if it roused them up.

A few black people, of course, were free. Some had been freed by a master grateful for outstanding service; others had purchased their freedom. But their liberty was limited at best. When they traveled, they had to carry papers proving that they were not runaway slaves, and sometimes unscrupulous whites would illegally force them back into slavery.

Among the freed black people was a Baptist preacher named George Liele, who conducted services at many points along the Savannah River in South Carolina and Georgia, and later on the island of Jamaica. Liele was probably the first ordained black Baptist pastor in America.

Our story, however, is not about Liele, but about a young slave named Andrew Bryan, whom Liele baptized at one of his preaching services near the Savannah River. The new convert soon demonstrated a gift for preaching and began to conduct services that were attended by both blacks and whites. One of those who was favorably impressed was Edward Davis of nearby Yamacraw. "How would you like to build a church on my land?" Davis asked Bryan one day. Delighted, of course, Bryan accepted the offer, and soon he and his friends had erected a simple wooden building.

Many of the slaveowners, however, were hostile. Even though Jonathan Bryan, Andrew's master whose family name he had taken, gave him every encouragement, others feared that the preaching would make the slaves discontented and rebellious. Exerting pressure against Davis, they forced Andrew Bryan's little congregation out of the building. Forbidden to hold regular meetings, the little flock had to "steal away to Jesus," conducting services secretly in the swamps, but in spite of this they held together and grew in their love and support for each other. When the Reverend Abraham Marshall came to the area in 1788, he baptized forty-five people, ordained Andrew Bryan to the Baptist ministry, and helped them to organize a church.

As the church grew stronger, persecution increased. Some of the whites formed vigilante patrols to stop the blacks and whip them when they were on their way to worship. Even those who carried written permits to travel, signed by their masters, were not safe. Some were arrested. Carter Woodson, a noted historian of the black church, quotes an old source when he says that Andrew Bryan and his brother Sampson were "inhumanly cut and their backs were so lacerated that their blood ran down to the earth as they, with uplifted hands, cried unto the Lord; but Bryan, in the midst of his torture, declared that he rejoiced not only to be whipped but would freely suffer death for the cause of Jesus Christ."

Andrew's master did all he could to help. He supported the two brothers at a court hearing, gained their release, and let them hold services in his barn. Even though spying and persecution by Andrew's white enemies continued, God used the spying in a remarkable way to help the little congregation. While some of them were eavesdropping outside the barn, they heard Andrew deliver such a moving prayer for God's mercy upon the persecutors that they withdrew and the persecution ceased. A judge ruled that the blacks might worship any time between sunrise and sunset. New friends arose among the white community, who contributed funds to purchase a lot in the city of Savannah and erect a real church building.

It seemed as though Andrew Bryan's problems were over—but not yet! Within a few years his master died, leaving Andrew still a slave and the church building still controlled by the family. At this point the whole enterprise could have fallen apart.

Fortunately, however, it didn't. Jonathan Bryan's heirs, remembering his love and appreciation for the Baptist preacher-slave, allowed Andrew to purchase his freedom for fifty pounds, a sum which was easily raised, and gave him permission to continue using the building. The church prospered and soon grew to seven hundred members. It became the mother of several other black churches as its influence spread across the state, and there was no further persecution in Bryan's lifetime.

Andrew Bryan's death in 1812 at the age of seventy-five was mourned by Christians both white and black throughout the area. A group of white Baptists, the Savannah Baptist Association, commemorated his passing with this flowery but sincere and well-deserved tribute:

The Association is sensibly affected by the death of the Rev. Andrew Bryan, a man of color and pastor of the First Colored Church in Savannah. This son of Africa, after suffering inexpressible persecutions in the cause of his divine Master, was at length permitted to discharge the duties of the ministry among his colored friends in peace and quiet, hundreds of whom, through his instrumentality, were brought to a knowledge of the truth as "it is in Jesus."

7

WILLIAM CAREY

"Expect . . . Attempt Great Things for God"

"See here, Carey! I don't want you spoiling any more of my leather!" Mr. Gotch exclaimed.

Young William Carey's mouth went dry, and his palms began to perspire. Being a shoemaker didn't bring in much money. All he earned was the cost of his labor as he worked with leather provided by the customer. Was he about to lose his best customer?

"How much money do you make in a week of cobbling shoes?" Gotch asked.

"About nine or ten shillings, sir."

"All right, then." Suddenly a twinkle shone in Gotch's eyes. "Suppose hereafter you concentrate on your Latin, Greek, and Hebrew, and I'll give you a weekly allowance of ten shillings so you'll be free to study."

Carey felt like exploding with joy. Gotch had noticed the Hebrew and Greek Testaments in the shop, but Carey had thought he disapproved. Instead, Gotch was going to make it possible for the young man to fulfill his dream of preparing for the Baptist ministry. With this amazing gift, a shrewd English businessman who recognized genius when he saw it started Carey on the road which makes him remembered even now, two centuries later.

But Carey was different from the other Baptist ministers. He had an idea deep inside himself that they did not share. From reading travel books and the Bible, he had become convinced that Christians ought to send missionaries to other parts of the world to tell people about Jesus Christ. This was an unpopular idea. Dr. Ryland, the minister who had baptized him, put his opposition in a few words: "When the Lord gets ready to convert the heathen, he will do it without your help or mine." But Carey could not be silenced. At a meeting attended by delegates from many churches he challenged them to break out of their small world and take the gospel message to distant lands.

"Lengthen your cords and strengthen your stakes," he pleaded, as he painted vivid pictures of the superstition, suffering, and ignorance of the multimillion heathen to whom no one offered the compassion of Christ. In simple eloquence he spoke words which are forever burned into the Christian conscience: *"Expect great things from God. Attempt great things for God."*

Thirteen people were sufficiently stirred that they held a meeting on the night of October 2, 1792. There in a room only ten by twelve feet in size they organized the first foreign missionary society of modern times and pledged $37 to finance the work. The leading spirit behind the movement was Carey's good friend and supporter, the Reverend Andrew Fuller, pastor of the Baptist church in Kettering. "We'll hold the ropes, William, if you'll go to India," Fuller promised. It was a historic day.

After many discouragements Carey, sustained more by faith than by any real sense of security, sailed for India. It was a stormy voyage. The little Danish sailing vessel was driven nearly to the coast of Brazil and almost wrecked off the Cape of Good Hope. In the five months of the voyage, it never passed another ship, nor did it land at any port until it dropped anchor in Calcutta harbor.

For William Carey there followed heartbreaking experiences of poverty almost to the point of starvation, of sickness in his family, and of the death of one of his children. He faced the opposition of his own British government, which tried to stop his missionary endeavors. The intellectual and literary leaders of England despised him. The influential *Edinburgh Review* sneered at him as "a consecrated cobbler, a delirious mechanic, and a didactic artisan."

For a time it seemed that his great enterprise of faith must fail. Carey, however, had too much dedication to quit. Only death could stop him—and it almost did, for his wife became mentally ill and attempted to kill him. Because so little financial support came from home, Carey was forced to seek secular employment.

Besides the torment of his personal problems, Carey suffered with outrage at the sight of the cruelties inflicted in those days in India upon women and children. He saw a young widow burned to death alongside the body of her dead husband. He wrote: "They tied her down with bamboo poles and piled dry leaves high above her, pouring melted preserved butter on top. Fire was put to the pile which immediately blazed very fiercely. No sooner was the fire kindled, than all the people set up a great shout. It was impossible to have heard the woman had she groaned or even cried aloud on account of the mad noise of the people, and it was impossible for her to stir or struggle on account of the bamboo poles which held her down like the levers of a press. We could not bear any more."

The indignant Carey went into action. He collected evidence showing that in six months in the Calcutta area alone, nearly three hundred widows had been burned to death—ten thousand in all of India. Carey bombarded the British government with persistent protests until by law on December 4, 1812, it banned these terrible murders.

So also Carey's blood boiled when he saw mothers hurling their female babies into the waters of the sacred Ganges River to drown because the babies might not get husbands in their own social class, or caste. Once more Carey vigorously protested and persuaded the government to stop these inhuman practices. There seemed to be no end to the atrocities he had to fight against. Appalled at the sight of lepers being burned alive, he promoted the founding of a lepers' hospital in Calcutta.

By now, he well understood that in preaching the gospel, a missionary had to work against every form of evil and injustice. His work required infinite patience, for he labored seven long years in order to win his first convert. When it finally came, the first conversion happened strangely and quickly. A Hindu, Krishna Pal, fell in some slippery mud on the river bank and suffered excruciating pain from a dislocated shoulder. Carey brought him to the mission, worked to relieve his pain, and preached the gospel to him. Three days before Christmas in the year 1800, Krishna Pal confessed Christ, broke bread, and joined with Carey in prayer. During the next week a mob of two thousand surrounded Krishna Pal's home, cursing, threatening, and finally dragging him to the judge who ordered him imprisoned. Carey secured his release and on December 28 had the great joy of leading his first convert into the river to be baptized. More than a thousand were to follow within a few years.

One day a ship arrived from England with great good news for Carey in a letter from a young printer and editor named William Ward. "I am coming to visit you," the letter said. "You once told me you would need someone to print the Scriptures—it is in my heart to live and die with you, to spend and be spent with you." With the arrival of the energetic young printer, great plans were made for printing the gospel. The two men even built their own paper mill, for without it no suitable paper was available; and Ward soon built a first-class printing plant and type foundry.

Assisted by capable and loyal associates like Joshua and Hannah Marshman, Carey worked feverishly to translate the Bible into the Bengali language, and one Sunday he triumphantly laid on the Communion table the first copy. It was an unforgettable day! In a few years the presses were turning out portions of the Bible translated by Carey in forty different languages and dialects, plus a hundred thousand tracts a year, and soon a Bengali dictionary of eighty thousand words.

In 1821 Carey and his fellow workers of the mission founded Serampore College, the first Christian college in Asia. The beautiful Greek-style building with its impressive columns was a monument which expressed the educational and spiritual objectives of the mission.

Dr. Carey's plan of self-support was so successful that at the end of his forty years' labor he had earned and contributed to the mission about $46,000 (which was much more valuable, of course, in those days than in ours). In all that time, the Baptist Missionary Society in Britain, which he had founded, had given him only $600 for the support of himself and his family.

There were tragedies, perils, and disappointments along with the triumphs. Three attempts were made to murder him. At one time there were five deaths in the mission within three months. A terrible fire destroyed the entire printing plant with all its plates, type, paper, and most of the manuscripts and translations. A cyclone shattered his beautiful garden. A flood swept away his home. A financial depression wiped out all the invested funds of the mission. His first wife went insane and died. His second wife also died. Baptists in Britain made false and malicious charges against him. And yet this wonderful, dedicated Christian survived and went on with his work until the morning on which he died.

William Carey had indeed expected great things from God and had achieved great things for God. He is known as the father of modern missions.

8

ANN and ADONIRAM JUDSON

Pioneer American Missionaries

As Deacon Hasseltine read the letter, his face reddened. "Sir, can you consent to part with your daughter early next spring, to see her no more in this world? Can you consent to her departure to a heathen land and her subjection to hardships and sufferings of a missionary life . . . to degradation, insult, persecution, and perhaps a violent death?" The letter came to its point, making an appeal which the good deacon could not resist: "Can you consent to all this for the sake of Him who left His heavenly home and died for her and for you?"

The writer was Adoniram Judson, a young theological student who was convinced that God wanted him to preach the gospel in India as William Carey was doing, something which no American had ever done before. The daughter was Ann Hasseltine, who shared his love, his dream, his calling. The father, doubtful though he was about such a venture, gave his consent. Even he could not foresee that the hardships which Judson predicted for Ann would indeed come true.

The young couple were married; Adoniram was ordained to the Christian ministry in the Congregational church; and the two set sail for Calcutta on February 19, 1812. It took until June to get there. During the long months at sea they read the Bible together day after day and from this experience came to an important decision. Standing on the deck, they talked about it.

"According to the New Testament," Adoniram said, "belief in Christ must come first, and *then* comes the ordinance of baptism. If we are to start a new colony of Christians, I'm now sure that it must be of the Baptist faith, for the Baptists are right, according to the Scriptures."

"I agree with you," Ann replied. "But the Congregationalists ordained you and sent you out here in good faith. How can you now decide that they are wrong and desert them to become a Baptist?"

The Congregationalists were willing to support them with prayers of encouragement and money as well, but in good conscience the Judsons decided they must break those ties. Ann wrote in a letter, "We feel that we are alone in the world with no real friend but each other, no one on whom we can depend but God." After their arrival in India, Ann and Adoniram were baptized in Calcutta by one of the British Baptists who were with William Carey. Coming up out of the water, Adoniram kissed his wife, saying, "My dear, you are the first American woman ever to go as a foreign missionary, and now we both are the first missionaries whom the Baptists of America have ever had among the heathen."

While in India they visited the famous English Baptist missionary William Carey, who advised them to go on to Burma. On July 2, 1813, they landed at Rangoon, sick and weak from a rough voyage that had taken them many days. They had nearly died. In fact, Ann was still so weak that she had to be carried.

It had been sixteen months since they had left Massachusetts, but now their mission began in a land of eight million people, some of them scattered in primitive villages through the jungles. Most were either Buddhists or animists (spirit worshipers), and they showed no signs of wanting a new religion. Besides the indifference of the people, there were snakes, scorpions, elephants, wildcats, centipedes, cobras, leopards, and tigers. Moreover, at that time Burma was an undeveloped land where life was cruel and unsafe and anything might happen. Disease was a constant threat.

Though at first they were lonely, isolated, and depressed, good news was on the way. A few months later the Judsons were cheered by word that the Baptists of America had taken them to their hearts and were sending money. Almost overnight, Baptists were stirred by the eloquent appeals of Luther Rice to organize missionary societies, and in 1814 a national society was formed which is now the Board of International Ministries of the American Baptist Churches in the U.S.A.

ANN AND ADONIRAM JUDSON

Like Carey, Judson found that winning his first convert to Christ in a new land was a slow work requiring patient endurance. On the road to the Shwe Dagon, the golden pagoda which was the pride of Rangoon's ten thousand people, Judson had built a thatched-roof hut with a front porch, where he would sit and invite tired travelers to rest awhile. There, engaging them in religious conversation, he would tell them about the one true God and his Son Jesus Christ. Among those who often came and listened was Maung Naw, who worked for a teakwood merchant. After six years, Maung Naw one day declared himself a disciple of Christ and was baptized in a large pond on Sunday, June 27, 1819. Others followed, and there in Rangoon Judson soon organized a little Baptist church of ten members.

The emperor now threatened to kill anyone who accepted the new religion. Therefore when Maung Ing, a fisherman, wanted to be baptized, Judson warned him that he risked his life. "Do you love Christ better than your own life?" he asked. The new convert replied that he did. Another who came was Maung Shwe Gaung, an old man who declared, "No one who really knows Christ can help loving him." Of such staunch converts Judson built the foundations of his mission in Burma.

Though the church had been established, the cost to Ann and Adoniram had been heavy. They had buried their first son, Roger, in a lonely grave. They had suffered from fever and had been exposed to cholera and other epidemics. They had been threatened with banishment. They had been robbed. They had been separated for seven months, during which false rumors of Judson's death had tormented Ann beyond description. But worse trials were to follow.

The Judsons moved to a place called Ava, near the emperor's seat of government, where Judson hoped to persuade the emperor to grant him liberty to preach the gospel freely. The emperor angrily rejected his plea.

War broke out between England and Burma while the Judsons were living in Ava. When the British fleet bombarded Rangoon, many foreigners were arrested as spies, and the Judsons fell under suspicion.

On a Tuesday in June, 1824, just as they were about to sit down to dinner, men pushed open the door and charged into their little home. Ann froze with horror at the sight of the lead man, Spotted

Face, a repulsive brute with two circles tattooed on his cheeks. He was a well-known criminal and was presently executioner at the prison, a sadist who enjoyed making others suffer. Spotted Face hurled himself at Judson, knocking the missionary to the floor, and dug his knees into the missionary's stomach. He tied Judson's arms behind his back and dragged him off to prison, while Ann tried in vain to obtain his release by offering money.

In the prison courtyard Judson's tormentors lifted his feet to a granite block and riveted upon them three pairs of ankle fetters. "Walk now, you teacher!" they taunted him. When he tried, he fell on his face. Next he was dragged into a cell without a window. The darkness, stifling hot, reeked with a nauseating stench. By the dim light from a small doorway Judson could discern some fifty naked prisoners around him. At night a long bamboo pole was slipped between his ankle fetters to hoist his feet so that only his shoulders and head rested on the floor. Rats and vermin plagued the prisoners, and Judson's hair and shoulders became smeared with slimy filth. His ankles were raw, chafed by the iron fetters, and the cord about his arms cut deeply into his flesh, which became infected.

After some days he was removed to the death house. There he lay upon his back with a 32-pound weight on his feet, which were again hoisted on a bamboo pole. The temperature was 100 degrees and the stench sickening. Talking was forbidden. Every day at three o'clock a gong sounded, and Spotted Face came in to lead some prisoner to his death.

Ann, who was pregnant, continued heroically while all this was happening. She used every trick she could think of to find a way to see her husband. Finally, by paying the government $100, she got permission to visit him. As she entered the prison, some ugly black birds which she could not identify crawled out of the murky darkness and frightened her. Spotted Face tried to order her out, but she walked courageously into the death house to see her husband.

Somehow she persuaded the governor to allow Judson and another imprisoned missionary to be moved into an open-sided shed where they could breathe a little fresh air. She managed to exchange notes with him in the spout of a teapot, filled with hot tea, which she was permitted to take to the prison daily. Later she was allowed to spend an hour visiting him in the shed.

Adoniram was greatly worried about the safety of his manuscript of the New Testament which he had translated into the Burmese language. It represented years of patient work. For safekeeping Ann had buried it in the garden back of their little home. Now Adoniram instructed her to dig it up and hide it in a pillow, "an old-looking pillow," he said, "so hard that no jailer would ever want to steal it." Thus he was able to have with him—sleeping on it—the only copy of the Burmese New Testament in the world.

With quiet heroism Ann continued to walk daily the two miles to the prison and the two miles returning. Each day she visited some government official with gifts and pleas for the release of the missionaries. The birth of her baby interrupted the visits, and shortly afterward she had a near-fatal disease. At the same time Adoniram also became ill with a terrible fever. Only the faithfulness of their Bengali cook, who carried food daily to both of them, saved their lives.

Finally the war ended and, with it, Judson's imprisonment. He and Ann returned to Rangoon to pick up the pieces and resume their ministry. But the saddest tragedy of all was yet to come. While Adoniram was away on a trip, the word reached him that his lovely and faithful Ann had died. Soon the baby died also, and Judson was left alone in a strange land.

Thus the story of Ann and Adoniram ends, but not the story of God's work in Burma. Adoniram Judson, after many months of deep depression, began his ministry again. By the year 1834 he had translated the entire Bible into Burmese. He had preached, baptized, built schools, and established mission stations. The number of converts grew into the hundreds. Eight years after Ann's death he married Sarah Boardman, who remained his wife until her death eleven years later, and after that there was a third wife, Emily Chubbuck—all remarkable women who greatly strengthened Judson in his work as it increased year after year until his death at sea on April 12, 1850.

The Burma mission of American Baptists continued until 1966, when the Burmese government ordered all missionaries to leave. But the mission had done its work well, and now there are estimated to be a quarter of a million Baptists in Burma, whose churches are organized into a strong Burma Baptist Convention.

9

JOHN MASON PECK

Church Builder of the West

West of the Alleghenies, the United States in the early 1800s was pioneer country. Families were pushing westward in covered wagons in search of land where they might establish their farms. The towns were the kind pictured in movies or television shows about the Old West—complete with saloons, dance-hall girls, and gun fights. Much of the land was still occupied by Indian tribes, and some of them were ready to fight to defend it against the encroachments of the white settlers. It was a rough-and-ready life, full of perils, and most people would say it was no place for a preacher.

But John Mason Peck did not agree. This Baptist minister in the Catskill Mountain country of New York State believed that preachers and churches were exactly what the West needed. "A large part of the American continent . . . is in darkness," he wrote in his diary. "In the United States there is an abundant field for missionary labor. How I should rejoice if Providence should open a door for my usefulness and labors in this way!"

The door began to open at a meeting where his friend Luther Rice was raising money to support the Judsons' heroic missionary work in Burma. Recognizing Peck's extraordinary abilities, Rice asked him to visit the Baptist churches of central New York State, pleading the cause of missions. Fund raising was not exactly what Peck had in mind, but he took over his new responsibility with almost furious energy, traveling 440 miles by horseback in the first three weeks, preaching nineteen times, and organizing missionary societies.

But the West was still calling, and Peck continued to press his original concern with Luther Rice. In a letter he wrote: "Is a permanent mission station in the West being planned? . . . Where would such a mission be located? . . . Would it be best to have schools connected with it? . . . And what education would a man require, to qualify for the job of western missionary?"

Rice responded warmly and with encouragement: "You will need a good English education and as much more as possible," he wrote. Besides this, Rice warned him that he who went West as a missionary must "go West for life."

Peck lost no time. Rushing to Philadelphia, he joined four fellow students in the only Baptist school available for training preachers. He drove himself to learn all he could in a single year—Latin, Greek, Hebrew, philosophy, theology, Bible, and English. He preached as often as he could; visited prisons, hospitals, and slums; met Baptist leaders; and laid plans for his great missionary journey to the West. Then he anxiously awaited the call.

Baptist delegates were gathering in Philadelphia for a national convention, and they would decide Peck's future. Would the delegates have the vision to accept the challenge, or would they turn down Peck's mission to the West? On the third day they voted to open a mission in the West, but whom would they send? On the fourth day the choice fell on Peck and a fellow student, James E. Welch.

In impressive services of dedication, Peck and Welch were publicly commissioned by prayer and the laying-on of hands to undertake this mission to the West. That night Peck wrote in his diary: "I have now put my hand to the plow. O Lord, may I never turn back—never regret this step. It is my duty to live, to labor, to die as a kind of pioneer in advancing the gospel."

Into a one-horse wagon, already piled high with bedding, food, a baby's crib, and a buffalo trunk, John Mason Peck loaded his family. His bonneted wife Sallie, with a baby in her arms and another "on the way," sat on the front seat while Eli and Hannah, the two older children, played in back. Peck climbed up beside her and slapped the reins over the horse's flanks. Away they went in the hot July sun, wagon wheels lurching over the narrow dusty road.

Eli, their firstborn, had played a most important part in the lives of John and Sallie Peck, more so than most babies do. It was his birth

50

that had led his parents, then Congregationalists, to many serious discussions about Bible teachings concerning baptism. Delaying his infant baptism while they decided, finally they had come to the Baptist position that only believers should be baptized. Together they had been baptized in a Catskill Mountain creek, and together they had dedicated themselves to a shared lifetime of service to God within the Baptist faith.

The wearying journey westward lasted 125 days as it followed poor roads and seldom-traveled trails through forests, across rivers, and over mountain passes. The hardships of the trip were so severe that when Peck crossed the Mississippi River to St. Louis on the little steamboat, he was too weak to walk or stand and had to be carried ashore on a stretcher. Sallie, expecting her new baby's birth within a few weeks, managed to summon up the strength to nurse her husband back to health.

St. Louis in those days was nothing like the present modern city, with its monumental Gateway Arch. But that arch symbolizes what the city was in pioneer days—the gateway to the West, the city where everybody gathered, the base for all expeditions into the prairies and beyond. It was a wild frontier settlement without a school or a church, but crowded with saloons, gambling dens, and trading posts. There were all kinds of people—trappers, traders, cowboys, Indians, hunters, settlers, gamblers, vagabonds, robbers, bums, and very, very few Christians. Here everything was so cramped that the whole Peck family was crowded into a single room.

Despite the problems, Peck and Welch rented the back of a store to serve as a combined school and preaching station. Thus began the first Baptist mission west of the Mississippi. A couple of months later they held a baptismal service on the river bank, immersing two converts. Within three years' time, Peck could count fifty day schools and Sunday schools that he had established in Illinois and Missouri. When he had arrived, the few school teachers available were hard-drinking, illiterate, untrained men who needed to be replaced. Wherever possible Peck found sober, well-trained persons to take their places. He brought the churches together in a common fellowship.

Finding that many of the migrant families had come West without Bibles, Peck organized the Missouri Bible Society. Through

51

mud and rain, snow and ice, he rode horseback, his saddlebags weighed down with Bibles and Christian tracts. He would knock at the doors of cabins in the wilderness and enter with a brisk, warmhearted greeting. He never left a cabin, however poor, without a gracious prayer and, if possible, without leaving a Bible as a gift.

With four children to care for, as well as the responsibilities of meal preparation and keeping the house in order, Sallie Peck must have wondered what her role was in the great mission to the West. She did what she could. She started in their home a Sunday school for black slave children. She nursed the sick when a plague of what was called prairie fever struck the community, taking the lives of her young son Eli and her own brother, who had come to live with them. Later, when John founded a theological seminary, she managed the kitchen and supervised the food budget. Always she was a loyal and supportive wife, willing and able to take care of things efficiently at home during John's long travels.

But there were many bitter disappointments for the Pecks. One of the first came when the school John had founded at St. Charles, twenty miles from St. Louis, was wrecked by the scandalous life of its headmaster, who proved to be a rogue. A worse calamity followed when the Baptist missionary society which had commissioned Peck as their missionary suddenly deserted him, having decided to concentrate all their resources on Judson's work in Burma. When this news reached Peck, he was flat on his back critically ill from overwork, long travels on horseback, and exposure to the hazards of weather and wilderness. For a year he suffered the loneliness of a rejected and penniless missionary, unable to understand why his fellow Baptists could not see the vast needs—and also the great future—of the West.

But God did not desert him. New friends arose as the Massachusetts Baptist Missionary Society made him their missionary and began to send him the lavish sum of $5 per week.

With this new support, Peck's work grew. He founded a college and a theological school in Illinois. He began a weekly religious journal called *The Western Pioneer*. He founded Sunday schools, missionary societies, and churches. He carried religious literature in his saddlebags, for he had a profound belief in the printed word. Together with Jonathan Going he created a plan for establishing on the North American continent a national society for missions, which today is the Board of National Ministries of the American Baptist Churches in the U.S.A. Later he served in Philadelphia as executive secretary of the American Baptist Publication Society, which is now the Board of Educational Ministries of the American Baptist Churches in the U.S.A. Harvard University gave him an honorary degree.

The old pioneer died at the age of seventy-nine, a veteran worn out in his Master's service. Baptists owned in him a master builder of extraordinary vision, enormous energy, and heroic stature. For his singleness of purpose and dedicated energy, God opened tremendous opportunities, and he made great use of them. May there be more of his kind!

10

WILLIAM KNIBB

Emancipator of Slaves

Mrs. Knibb tore open the letter from her son. It was the first that William had written since leaving England in November, 1824, to take up the mission work on the lovely tropical island of Jamaica after his brother's death had left a great vacancy there. The letter brought good news and bad news. William and his young bride had arrived safely after their voyage across the Atlantic and had found the schoolhouse where brother Tom had taught, but it was almost a complete wreck. A new one would have to be built. Worse than that, William was shocked at the conditions he found among the black slaves who were the chief inhabitants of the island. "The cursed blast of slavery has, like a pestilence, withered almost every moral bloom. For myself, I feel a burning hatred against it as one of the most odious monsters that ever disgraced the earth."

Rebuilding the schoolhouse was a challenge, but it was quickly accomplished. Next, Knibb built a girls' school close by. Then he reopened his brother's chapel at Port Royal, and soon such crowds were coming to church that there was not room enough for them all. He enlarged the building. Traveling about the island, he drew the scattered Baptists into an organization known as the Jamaica Baptist Association. Often as many as a thousand people would attend his meetings.

But they were a very troubled people. Knibb saw that converting them to Christ was not enough, for he must rid the island of slavery if he were to preach the gospel in its fullness. Fearlessly he expressed his indignation against the brutality of the slave owners and declared that all slavery should be abolished as indecent and unchristian.

Naturally the slaveholding planters, who were enriching themselves at the expense of the slaves' misery, went into prompt action against this young intruder. It was not the job of a missionary to stir up discontent, they said, but rather to keep the slaves contented and happy in their gospel meetings. The slaveholders got a commission appointed to "investigate" the missionaries and persuaded the newspapers to publish vicious lies accusing the missionaries of stirring up rebellion, of extorting money from the slaves, and even of persuading women to sell their bodies to finance the mission. They sent thousands of copies of these lies back to England.

Here is an example of what was happening. Sam Sidney, a converted slave and deacon in the Baptist church, was arrested for praying publicly at a gathering in Knibb's home. He was forced to lie on the ground, naked, held down by four men, while twenty lashes with a bull whip were inflicted upon his bleeding back. He then was chained and made to walk in the hot sun to the fields for two weeks' hard labor as a member of a chain gang. Alongside Sam Sidney walked William Knibb, hand in hand, assuring him of God's grace.

When Knibb became pastor of a 900-member Baptist church in Falmouth, Jamaica, the angry planters renewed their war, denouncing the missionaries in public meetings as "infuriated lunatics." Some declared that they would kill their slaves rather than grant them freedom, and news of this threat caused some of the slaves to revolt. All of this, of course, was blamed on Knibb. His friends urged him to escape from the island while he still could, but he refused. At last the storm of opposition struck full force as Knibb was arrested and imprisoned. His chapels and schools were wrecked and burned, as also were the homes of the Baptist slaves. Finally a law was passed forcing the mission to close.

But imprisonment gave William Knibb an opportunity to think out a determined plan of action. He resolved not to rest until he had fought the slaveholders to a finish and had freed every one of the thirty thousand slaves on the island. To accomplish this, he would have to return to England and get Parliament to pass a law. As soon as his prison term ended, therefore, he hurriedly sailed for England. It was a close call, for twenty conspirators had taken an oath that they would kill him as soon as he was freed from jail. But God spared him. Landing in England in 1832 at the age of twenty-nine, Knibb met with the executive committee of the Baptist Missionary Society. At first they advised him to forget it. Slavery was a political issue, they said, and the Missionary Society should convert sinners, not get involved in politics. In answer, Knibb rose to his feet, looked the committee chairman in the eye, and declared: "My wife, my children, and I are entirely dependent on the Baptist mission. We have landed here without a shilling, but if necessary I will take my wife and children by the hand and I will walk barefoot throughout the length and breadth of the United Kingdom to make known to the Christians of England what their brethren in Jamaica are suffering."

A few days later he attended the annual meeting of the Missionary Society, for which a great crowd had gathered. He heard many earnest sermons and emotional appeals for noble causes, but never a reference to the curse of slavery. His muscles quivered as he felt the pain of his black brothers in Jamaica who at that very moment were being flogged and were seeing their homes burned as punishment for their faith.

Knibb rose to speak. A nearby pastor tried to stop him. Knibb persisted. "I *will* speak!" he shouted. "At the risk of the severing of my connection with the society and the loss of all I hold dear, I will avow this, and if the friends of missions will not hear me, I will turn and tell it to my God! Nor will I desist till this greatest of all curses is removed and 'Glory to God in the highest!' is inscribed on the British flag."

For two years he waged a one-man campaign to arouse public opinion against slavery in Jamaica. He traveled the length and breadth of England and Scotland conducting public rallies. His zeal and eloquence roused vast numbers of people in support of his cause. Audiences gave him deafening applause. Often he was accompanied by Eustace Carey, a nephew of William Carey, the pioneer Baptist missionary. Eustace Carey wrote: "I witnessed congregated masses burning and almost raving with indignation at the slave system, as Knibb depicted its cruelties and demonstrated its crimes."

The campaign was successful. The British Parliament enacted a law abolishing colonial slavery and set midnight of July 31, 1833, as the hour when the slaves should become legally free. Parliament also agreed to pay a large sum of money toward the rebuilding of the chapels, churches, and homes that had been destroyed in Jamaica. A few years later, Parliament also voted to make payments to the planters to help them bear the financial burdens which the liberation of their slaves created for them. All of this happened many years before Abraham Lincoln issued the Emancipation Proclamation in the United States which freed the slaves in the South.

Of course, that midnight of July 31, 1833, had to be a time of great celebration on the island of Jamaica, and William Knibb wasn't about to miss it. He was welcomed back with tremendous enthusiasm by the black population, amid scenes of indescribable joy and affection. The planters, of course, did not share this exuberance, but Knibb stood there on that joyous night surrounded by a vast throng of black Jamaicans. As the midnight hour arrived, he cried out: "The monster is dead! You are free! Thanks be to God!"

Shortly afterward, William Knibb was stricken by yellow fever. The attack proved fatal, and although he died at the early age of forty-two, he had achieved more than do most men in twice that number of years.

11

LOTT CAREY

First Black Missionary to Africa

Granny Mihala cuddled the little black child against her as once again she told him the old story. "Our people came from far away, Lott, across a great water called the ocean, from a land called Africa, where they lived in freedom. But slave traders brought them to America to work in the fields."

"What was it like in Africa, Granny?" Lott asked.

"Well, it's been a long time, and I wish I knew more to tell you, but some things I do know. Africa is very beautiful, with jungles and strange animals that we don't see here in Virginia and little villages where black people live together in peace without white masters to tell them what to do."

Lott climbed into Granny's arms. "How far is it to Africa?" he asked.

"Many, many days by boat, Lott," she replied. "Maybe a hundred. It is a terrible trip. Many black people died on the way here. They were packed in so tight, and the air was bad and the food was bad, and so many were sick."

"Do the folks in Africa know about Jesus, Granny?"

"No, Lott, I don't reckon they do. Our people didn't learn about Jesus till they came to Virginia. A lot of bad things happened to us here, but that was one of the good things. Many of the people in Africa worship spirits."

"And do all of them think that the great God lives far away from them and does not love them?"

"No, Lott, because they do not even know about our God.

BAPTISTS WHO DARED

Sometimes I wish I could go back to Africa and tell them, but I am too old. Perhaps it may be you who will travel over the big seas to carry the great secret to my people. Mihala will be dust, but her prayers will live that your feet may find the path, and after you, others of our race—hundreds of them!"

As Lott grew older, he remembered Mihala's words. Though a slave, he was more fortunate than many, because his family stayed together, unlike many families that were broken up by the sale of some of their members to other masters. Having no brothers or sisters, the boy was very close to the older people, not only Mihala but his parents as well, especially his strong, rugged, God-fearing father.

When Lott was twenty-four, his master sent him to the city of Richmond to work in a tobacco warehouse. There, like many young men away from home for the first time, young Carey began to drink too much, swear too much, and run around too much. But something about his early training must have told him this was the wrong kind of life, for after two or three years he turned to Christ. His conversion occurred at the First Baptist Church, where he heard a particularly stirring sermon about Nicodemus. Lott confessed his faith, was baptized, and joined the church.

The story of Nicodemus, who came to Jesus by night and learned from him what it meant to be born again, made a deep impression on Lott Carey. Wanting to read the story for himself, the illiterate youth, with some help, taught himself to read and write. He then enrolled in night school, where he studied reading, writing, arithmetic, the Bible, current events, and even some economics. Soon he was promoted to supervisor in the warehouse and earned enough money to buy his freedom. As his activity in the church increased, he felt called to the Christian ministry. The First Baptist Church licensed him to preach, and he began to deliver sermons all over Virginia—eloquent sermons that stirred people deeply.

But there was an even deeper call yet to come, and this reached him through William Crane, his night-school teacher. Deeply interested in the idea of Christian missions in Africa, Crane made frequent speeches on this subject, which also became a theme of much of Carey's preaching. As a result the Richmond African Missionary Society was formed, with Lott Carey as one of its chief spokesmen and supporters. Finally Mihala's grandson fulfilled her dream by declaring his call to become the first black missionary to Africa. "I am an African," he said, "and in this country [America], however meritorious my conduct, and respectable my character, I cannot receive the credit due to either. I wish to go to a country where I shall be estimated by my merits, not by my complexion; and I feel bound to labor for my suffering race. . . . I long to preach to the poor African the way of life and salvation."

With the help of many Baptists, both black and white, the mission was made possible, and Lott Carey with six others constituting his "missionary church" sailed from Norfolk for Sierra Leone, West Africa, on January 23, 1821. "I don't know what may befall me," he had said in a sermon shortly before his departure, "whether I may find a grave in the ocean, or among the savage men, or more savage wild beasts on the coast of Africa, nor am I anxious what may become of me. I feel it my duty to go."

Freetown, the capital of Sierra Leone, deserved its name, for the British had abolished the slave trade in 1807 and had made the city a place of refuge for liberated black people. About twelve hundred former slaves were living there when Carey arrived, and colonization projects which would bring more were developing in America and Britain.

There were more disappointments than achievements, however, in those first years overseas. An American colony for freed slaves, which Carey had intended to make the nucleus of his mission, failed to materialize. Carey's second wife died (his first had died in Virginia), leaving him with the responsibility of three children. Political red tape seemed to present impossible obstacles.

Nevertheless, progress was made as the little missionary church he had transplanted from America took root and held its first Communion service on African soil. Carey began to preach in various parts of Africa and established a mission among the Mandingoes, the tribe later made famous through the popular book *Roots*. The American Colonization Society purchased lands which would later become the Republic of Liberia, and Lott Carey was appointed to the transitional government as Health Officer and Government Inspector.

The new nation-to-be had to fight for its existence against warring tribes. Land had to be cleared for settlement and cultivation.

Severe economic, political, and health problems arose. Conflict developed between Carey's group and Jehudi Ashmun, the colonial manager, who stopped their rations because they would not cooperate with his policies. When they retaliated by seizing their rations from the storehouse, Ashmun barred Carey from performing his ministerial functions, but Carey soon made his peace with Ashmun, and the restrictions were lifted.

Still a colony, with Ashmun now as its governor, Liberia began to develop, and Carey began to build schools and churches. Though he never had any formal medical training, he studied medical books privately, learning to treat many kinds of illnesses and injuries, and established a medical mission. He also developed a health plan for slaves emigrating from America to Liberia, including a schedule indicating the best months for them to travel and settle in order to minimize the shock of moving to a tropical climate. He became vice-agent of the colony, then temporarily took complete charge when Ashmun left the country, and finally was appointed governor upon Ashmun's death in 1828.

A year later, however, tribal warfare again broke out, and the colony had to defend itself against native raids. Carey and a group of friends were killed by an explosion while manufacturing cartridges to be used in the colony's defense.

Liberia today is a free Christian nation on the west coast of Africa, with more than twenty thousand Baptists among its citizens. One of its most distinguished leaders has been President William R. Tolbert, Jr., who served also as president of the Baptist World Alliance from 1965 to 1970. Thus the little missionary church of Lott Carey has grown and produced much good fruit.

12

JOHANN GERHARD ONCKEN

Pioneer German Baptist Pastor

Johann Gerhard Oncken stood at the rail of the sailing vessel as it slowly entered Hamburg harbor. "My native Germany," he pondered. "Once again I will live among my own people, and I will help them to know Jesus Christ."

It had been ten years since Oncken, now a young man of twenty-three, had left his hometown of Varel, some eighty miles west of Hamburg, to live in Scotland as an apprentice to a tradesman who had taken a liking to him. His Scottish master, a devout Presbyterian, had insisted that the young Lutheran boy have a Bible of his own and read it regularly. Johann had prized his Bible dearly.

The turning point of his life, however, came when he was nineteen. Riding on the top of a London-bound stagecoach, he was abruptly thrown to the ground when the coach gave a lurch, and he lay in the street bleeding from his mouth and nose. This sudden encounter with near-death made him sensitive to the prayers of the London family with whom he stayed, as they audibly pleaded with God that the young man might be converted. Their prayers were answered. After hearing a particularly rousing sermon in the Methodist church, Johann fully accepted Christ as Savior and Lord. In fact, so complete was his conversion that he immediately began to think of becoming a missionary. "From that day I became a witness, albeit a weak one, of God's love to sinners and of his all-powerful grace," he later wrote. Burning with enthusiasm, Johann Oncken betook himself to Germany as a missionary of the British Continental Society.

BAPTISTS WHO DARED

The official German state church was Lutheran, and the preaching of other brands of Christianity was disapproved, but young Oncken now found the Lutheran faith of his boyhood lacking in the evangelical spirit, the freedom, the biblical witness that he wanted. He preferred the Presbyterianism he had known in Scotland or the Methodism he had experienced in England, but these faiths were not to be found in Germany. Finally, he became a member of the English Reformed Church and set out to witness for Christ in Hamburg. The Lutherans, of course, opposed him, and so he had to do his preaching in cellars, garrets, and alleys.

Everywhere he went, he distributed Bibles. Once, when he sent a messenger to the supply depot for more Bibles, the Lutheran minister in charge asked, "What becomes of all these Bibles? Does the man eat them? He shall have no more." So Oncken himself went to the depot to get the Bibles. There he was greeted with an outburst of temper: "So, *you* are the man who preaches in the cellars, garrets, and everywhere! Your cursed preaching! Whoever told you to preach?" With spirit Oncken replied, "The Lord Jesus has commanded me to preach!" The state minister sprang to his feet and retorted, "The devil has commanded you."

Eventually Oncken was forbidden to preach, and he then saw that more than ever he must resort to the power of the printed gospel and the distribution of Bibles. In 1828 he became an agent for the Edinburgh Bible Society, and in his lifetime he printed and distributed more than two million copies of the Bible. He opened a bookstore in his home and established a print shop and a successful publishing business still known among Baptists in Germany as the Oncken Verlag (or Oncken Press).

How did this Lutheran-Presbyterian-Methodist-Reformed Bible preacher become a Baptist? It happened simply enough. When Oncken and his wife welcomed the first baby into their home, he began to wonder whether it was biblical to have the infant christened. Finally becoming convinced that there was no authority in the Scriptures for infant baptism, he accepted believers' baptism as the true New Testament concept. But he had a problem. Though now a Baptist by conviction, he could not find a Baptist minister in all of Germany to baptize him. It took five years for him to find one.

It was Professor Barnas Sears, of Hamilton Literary and

Theological Institution in the United States, who was studying in Europe in 1834, who finally responded to Oncken's desire and baptized him along with six others in the river Elbe. They had to come secretly by night to the chosen spot, for they risked having their property seized by the officers and even being sent to prison. In a boat that was waiting for them at the riverside they were quietly rowed to a lonely, secluded island. "Although externally all was dark, within us was light," Oncken later recalled.

Now began a campaign by the authorities to stop Oncken's work by either bribery or persecution. At first he was offered the alluring gift of a free passage to the United States for himself and the members of his family if only he would get out of Germany and stay far away. This he refused.

Because he refused, the expected happened; he was thrown into the Winserbaum State Prison in Hamburg. The dark and clammy prison cell was an unsanitary place, washed on two sides by a stream of sewage which filled the air with an unwholesome stench. Consequently Oncken caught a disease which caused him lifelong suffering.

Oncken's prison, like John Bunyan's, stood close beside a bridge. One of his earliest converts, a scholarly Jew and son of a rabbi, Köbner by name, was imprisoned in a cell located just above Oncken's. When Köbner began to sing a hymn, Oncken recognized his voice, and together they joined in singing praise to God in the dark prison. Some of Oncken's church congregation gathered on the bridge beside the prison to wave to him and cheer him, but they were soon scattered by the police and dared not meet again except secretly in little groups.

Oncken suffered numerous imprisonments and lived constantly under the threat of sudden arrest. One day when he was with a few friends in a public garden on the shore of the river Elbe, an unknown woman approached him and whispered in his ear: "Mounted soldiers are at the garden park gate waiting to take you prisoner as you leave." Quickly Oncken jumped over a hedge and dashed downhill to the river where he found a friend with a boat. "You are sent by the Lord to help me escape to Hamburg!" he cried, leaping into the boat which carried him away to safety.

Meanwhile, the work of the Baptists advanced as it always has done under persecution. The First Baptist Church, which Oncken had established in Hamburg in 1834 with only seven members, had by this time grown to a congregation of several hundred and now owned a four-story building which had once been a warehouse but was now their place of worship. American Baptists appointed Oncken as their organizing missionary in Germany and throughout Europe and continued to support him for many years. Little did they realize that the grandson of one of his converts would come to the United States a century later as a refugee from the Nazis who had tried to block him from the preaching of his Baptist witness in Germany. This man, Herbert Gezork, was to become the president of an American Baptist theological school (Andover Newton) and the president of the national organization now known as the American Baptist Churches in the U.S.A.

The persecution of Baptists in Hamburg was halted temporarily by a disastrous fire which, in 1842, left a third of the city in ruins. Pastor Oncken, without delay, opened three stories of the Baptist church building as a place of refuge for the homeless. For a time after this act of mercy, the people of Hamburg were less interested in persecuting the Baptists.

Nevertheless, in time even this was forgotten, and before persecution finally ended, Oncken was twice more imprisoned at Winserbaum. It was not until 1860 that a law was passed giving full religious freedom to all denominations. It was a great day for Oncken, on April 17, 1867, when he dedicated the new First Baptist Church in Hamburg, a beautiful building seating a congregation of 1,400 persons.

Oncken's witness was not limited to Germany. He carried his work into Denmark, where he founded the First Baptist Church of Copenhagen, and into the Netherlands, where he also founded a Baptist church. He preached in Lithuania, Switzerland, Poland, Russia, and other countries.

In Germany the Baptist churches spread across the country, and by the time of Oncken's death in 1884 there were many thousands of Baptists as well as a theological seminary and a strong publishing house to bear witness to the faith. The inscription placed by the Hamburg church upon his gravestone eloquently called him their "never-to-be-forgotten pastor."

13

ELLEN WINSOR CUSHING

Educator with a World Vision

Ellen Winsor loved excitement. As a child she had heard her mother tell stories of Ann and Adoniram Judson, the pioneer missionaries to Burma, and she too had longed to go in Christian service to some faraway place. But there had been no opportunities. Now, teaching school in Boston at the age of twenty-one, it looked as though hers would be a quiet and conventional life.

Then, in 1861, war broke out—the bloody conflict between North and South that tore America apart. As ships of the United States Navy moved swiftly along the coast of South Carolina capturing the rich cotton plantations, the plantation owners fled to safety. Their black slaves, left behind without supervision or guidance, were in terrible trouble. They did not know how to go about providing food and clothing to keep themselves alive, and, of course, they did not know how to read or write, because education of slaves was forbidden.

South Carolina became Ellen's Burma. Unable to go overseas, she found a mission for her life by responding to the challenge of Salmon P. Chase, secretary of the treasury, who was recruiting young people from northern cities to supervise the deserted plantations. Ellen, as part of a group known as Gideon's Band, went to South Carolina, and there was placed in charge of Pope's Plantation.

In short order she demonstrated that she had a great talent for organization. As a young woman doing the work of an older man in a time when women just didn't do things like that, she set the plantation in order. Soon the workers were back in the fields, and the tasks of planting, weeding, and harvesting were going forward efficiently. Ellen, however, was interested in more than this, for she wanted to change the system by which the slaves were deliberately kept in ignorance. She wanted them to learn the value of money, so that they might be able to manage their lives effectively when their inevitable freedom would come. So she began to pay them wages—something the plantation owners had never done—and thus the slaves learned to buy the things they needed. And the children? Ellen was still a school-teacher at heart. When she saw the slave children who had never had the privilege of education in any form, she set up a school and became their teacher. Revolutionary!

Life in South Carolina wasn't easy for Ellen. For one thing, being unaccustomed to the climate, she caught the dread disease known as yellow fever. For ten days she was unconscious while her new friends, the slaves, tenderly nursed her back to health.

More than this, she was a stranger in enemy territory. Ellen represented the Union, and South Carolina was at war with the Union. To defend her plantation and the work she was doing, therefore, she obtained a commission as a captain in the United States Army— almost a century before the army was regularly opened to women— and organized a company of one hundred men, whom she trained as a fighting force. A strange army indeed was Captain Ellen's little force, composed of field hands and refugees who had never before even dreamed of themselves as soldiers, but they garrisoned the plantation and protected it.

On one occasion she encountered a man, dressed as a Union naval officer, with a squad of enlisted men. Something about him, especially the questions he asked, aroused her suspicions. Cleverly she invited him to be her dinner guest; and while he was at the plantation, she telegraphed the United States Army headquarters to check him out. Sure enough, her guest was a Confederate spy, and it was Captain Ellen who captured him.

While all this was going on, she found time for romance. On another plantation lived J. Milton Fairfield, who like herself was working with the slaves to help them become more self-reliant. She fell in love with him, and they were married, but the marriage was short-lived, for he lost his life in a shipwreck two years later.

With the coming of peace, the young widow returned to Boston,

where her restless and compassionate desire to help others led her to a new vocation. Her heart went out to the many street children of Boston. In those days, if a child's parents died, and there was nobody else to care, the orphan lived in the streets by begging and stealing. To meet this need, there was being organized in Boston the Home for Little Wanderers, a place where these parentless children might be cared for. To Ellen this was another opportunity to serve God by helping humanity. She was placed in charge of the new home for children, and there she served for about a year.

But there was to be a second love in Ellen's life, and with it the much-hoped-for call to Burma. In nearby Newton a young man named Josiah Cushing, who was studying for the ministry and wanted to go to Burma as a missionary, was looking for a wife to go with him. This was just what Ellen had been hoping for, and she was attracted both to Josiah and to his plans. They were married on her twenty-sixth birthday and shortly thereafter sailed for that distant land.

Josiah and Ellen gave outstanding service in the Burma mission, and to this day they are held in honored memory by the Baptists of that nation. So eager were the Cushings to maximize their ministry that for periods of time they lived separately, he in one mission station and she in another, so as to double their effectiveness.

But Burma's climate, like South Carolina's, was too much for Ellen's fragile health. Within a few years she became so ill that she had to return to the United States, leaving Josiah alone to continue a great and heroic missionary career in Burma. From that time on, Ellen was to see her husband only when he returned home on furloughs, at seven-year intervals. During this period she continued her ministry by speaking before church groups, raising money to support the mission, and urging young people to select missionary service as a career. She started a school in Philadelphia, known during her lifetime as the Baptist Institute for Christian Workers, and much later as Cushing Junior College, which for many years helped young women to prepare themselves for significant Christian work in the church or elsewhere in the world. "Woman in her best estate is not only educated and refined but practical," she declared.

This might well have been the end of her story. Ellen might have continued teaching young women until she retired, and then she might have spent her last years knitting by the fire. But it wasn't that way. At the age of sixty-five—old enough to retire, by many standards—she was shocked by the sudden death of her husband, who collapsed at the platform after delivering a missionary address at the Northern Baptist Convention in St. Louis. His funeral, held at the close of the convention, was attended by Baptist leaders already gathered from all over the world.

Josiah's death presented Ellen with a challenge to still another career. He hadn't expected to die. He had left unfinished a translation of the New Testament into the Shan language, one of the many tongues of Burma, as well as the compilation of a Shan grammar and dictionary. Somebody had to go back to Burma and finish the job—who else but Ellen? So she went back once more to the land of her girlhood dreams, the Burma where she had ministered so many years ago, the Burma which her health could not tolerate. For three years she worked over Josiah's manuscripts, until they were completed and the printer's copy was ready. Finally, an eye infection forced her to return to the United States.

Even then, at the age of sixty-eight, Ellen Cushing did not retire to knitting by the fireside. For seven more years she traveled incessantly around the country, speaking in behalf of her school and the Burma mission. She loved to speak, and the people loved to hear her. Appropriately enough, her death occurred at Providence, Rhode Island, where she had gone at the age of seventy-five to deliver a missionary address at the First Baptist Church—the church which Roger Williams had founded almost three centuries earlier to start the Baptist movement in America, the church where she herself had been baptized as a young girl.

14

JOHN E. CLOUGH

Friend of the Outcastes

On an Iowa farm in the 1860s a young man was standing on a four-horse reaper breaking off the heavy grain when one of the farmhands came across the field calling out, "Here's a letter for you from Boston!" John Clough seated himself on the reaper, tied the reins around the seat, and tore open the letter. As he read, his eyes widened with surprise. Then a broad smile came upon his face. "What do you know!" he shouted. "They want me to go to India as a missionary! It's a call from the Baptist Foreign Mission Board in Boston."

John Clough was more than a farmer. He was an educated man who had been head of a public school and had served as a leader in politics. More recently he had felt called to religious service and had been distributing literature for the American Baptist Publication Society in the Midwest. It was at a Baptist Convention in Davenport, Iowa, that an address by a missionary to Thailand had stirred him to apply for appointment to the overseas mission field himself.

Clough had not always been a Christian. In college he had been greatly annoyed with a roommate who insisted on reading the Bible and praying aloud. Clough had insisted on drawing a line down the center of the room with the understanding that all praying would be done on the other side of it and he could do as he pleased on his side. One evening, however, the president of the university had persuaded him to attend a service at the Baptist church, and the experience had moved Clough deeply. Returning to his dormitory room, he stepped across the chalk line and knelt beside his praying roommate.

Clough's missionary assignment in India was to work among the Telugu people, a field which was known as the Lone Star Mission, or sometimes "The Forlorn Hope," because it had enjoyed so little success since its establishment a quarter of a century earlier. Three times the mission board had considered closing it. The final decision to keep it open had been made as a result of an appeal through poetry by the Reverend Samuel F. Smith, who was also the author of "My Country 'Tis of Thee." The final stanza of Smith's poem about the Lone Star Mission won the Board to its support:

> Shine on, "Lone Star!" till earth redeemed
> In dust shall bid its idols fall;
> And thousands, where thy radiance beamed,
> Shall "crown the Saviour, Lord of all."

So this, a decade later, was Clough's challenge—to bring thousands to the Savior in a mission where scarcely any had responded in the past.

On November 30, 1864, therefore, John E. Clough and his brave wife, Harriet, set sail from Boston on a little ship called the *James Guthrie*. Scarcely seaworthy, the *Guthrie* rolled and pitched unmercifully and narrowly missed drifting into the wreckage of old ships as it rounded the Cape of Good Hope.

They did not arrive in India until almost the first of April. Then they journeyed by slow stages on a springless oxcart to the mission station at Nellore and on to Ongole, where they were to open a new station. There at a place known as Prayer Meeting Hill because of a service held there by another missionary ten years earlier, Clough began his work.

In the area around Ongole lived a great many people known as Madigas, who were outcastes in the complicated social system of India at that time. In that system there were many social classes, or castes, into which persons were born, and which everyone observed with the utmost strictness. The mixing of persons of differing castes was severely limited, and the outcastes, who were at the very bottom of the ladder, were scorned and despised by everybody else. These Madiga outcastes had been hearing about Christ and were interested in coming to the mission, but Clough knew that to accept them would cost him the friendship of the community's "best people."

It was a difficult decision, and it took a brave man to make it. The people of the higher castes, who would be desirable additions to the church, let Clough know that they would not become Christians if they would have to associate with the outcastes, who (among other repulsive practices) were accustomed to eating carrion, or putrefied dead animals, especially cows, which no good Hindu would eat.

"Must I forbid the outcaste people to come to Christ in order to receive into membership some of the high caste people?" Clough asked himself. Then a strange thing happened. As Clough prayed for understanding, he opened his Bible at random, and the text of 1 Corinthians 1:26-29 was before his eyes. At almost the same time in another room Harriet Clough opened her Bible and her eyes fell on precisely the same text. In the King James Version, which was the only one available to most English-speaking people in those days, this is what they read:

> For ye see your calling, brethren, how that not many wise men after the flesh, not many mighty, not many noble, are called:
> But God hath chosen the foolish things of the world to confound the wise; and God hath chosen the weak things of the world to confound the things which are mighty;
> And base things of the world, and things which are despised, hath God chosen, yea, and things which are not, to bring to nought things that are:
> That no flesh should glory in his presence.

Clough interpreted this double event as more than coincidence. He felt that the Lord had spoken to him. "The foolish . . . the weak . . . the base . . . the things which are despised. . . ." These terms described the outcastes exactly. There was only one course to take. Clough rejected the caste system, declaring that segregation had no place in the Baptist church of India. The outcastes were to be welcome to come to Christ, as were people of every caste, with the understanding that all are one in Christ Jesus. This historic decision brought converts by the hundreds, most of them outcastes. Clough felt sure that he had done the right thing.

He insisted that the Madigas, as a test of their faith, should make three changes in their way of life. First, they must observe Sunday as a holy day. Second, they must stop eating carrion, and third, they must refrain from pagan ceremonies. All three of these demands created problems in the community: the first, because their employers wanted them to work on Sunday; the second, because there were now many dead cows lying around; and the third, because the outcastes could no longer be the village entertainers. Thus the Madigas found themselves under great tension. Clough himself was placed under great pressure by the leading citizens, first because he had violated the caste system but now also because he had created conflict between the once servile outcastes and their "betters."

But Clough survived these problems and went on to deal with others. In the years of 1876–1878, India suffered from a great famine. With the compassion of the Christ who fed the five thousand, he threw all his energies into feeding the hungry with the help of money raised through his appeals in England and the United States. To help the people earn money to buy the scarce and expensive food that was available, he contracted with the British Government to build a four-mile irrigation canal, thus providing many jobs.

During rest periods on the canal project, native preachers serving as overseers read the Bible to the workers and taught them the gospel. Many of the natives, moved by this preaching and convinced of Clough's sincerity by his works of mercy, desired to become Christians. For fifteen months, Clough refused to baptize them, for he did not want "rice Christians" (that is, people who accepted Christ insincerely in order to get food). Not until he had examined each of them personally and become convinced of their sincerity did he accept them for baptism. Their response convinced him so completely that he could no longer hold them back.

Accordingly, Clough one day stood under a grove of trees on the river bank and supervised his ordained native preachers as they baptized great numbers of people. That was a day never to be forgotten. The baptizing started at 6 A.M., and by 5 P.M. the number of persons immersed had reached 2,222. They continued to baptize for the next two days until the total reached 3,536 Indian converts, more than were baptized on the day of Pentecost.

The next year, Clough and his helpers toured among the villages and continued their baptizing. In 39 days they baptized a total of 8,691 persons. During this time Clough also ordained 24 Telugu preachers. So amazing was the revival movement that there were 20,865 Christians connected with the Ongole field by the year 1882, less than twenty years after Clough had begun his work. To this day Ongole remains an important Baptist center in South India, including a secondary school, a junior college, a hospital, a clinic, and a boarding home among its facilities—all because John Clough had the courage to begin by accepting the outcastes.

15

WALTER RAUSCHENBUSCH

Prophet of Social Justice

Young Walter Rauschenbusch faced the bitter truth. Obviously he was mistaken in the notion that God wanted him to go to India as a missionary. This was abundantly clear from the fact that the Baptist mission society had turned down his application. When God wants you to do something, Walter reasoned, God shows you the way and opens the door. Well, perhaps there would be something else.

Walter's life already contained many interesting memories that had helped to shape his destiny. Born on October 4, 1861, he had been old enough to experience the terrible shock which swept across the land at the assassination of Abraham Lincoln. He could remember visiting Germany as a boy and feeling some of the richness of his ancestral heritage. He could recall laboring as a schoolboy on vacation in the intense midsummer heat of a Pennsylvania farm from sunup to sundown, for the munificent sum of 25 cents per day.

But most of all he could remember vividly the decisive hours of his life which occurred at age seventeen when he was facing the problems of growing into manhood. Fervently he had prayed for help and in return had experienced a deep, tender, and mysterious response from the Lord which, he declared, influenced his soul down to its depths. Convinced that God had a special mission for his life, he decided to enter the Baptist ministry and in preparation studied at the University of Berlin and the Rochester Theological Seminary. Through these experiences he felt himself growing into a sensitive, deeply religious man who loved Christ and cared about people, especially the poor.

Why, then, had the door to India been closed to him? India had so many poor people and such great need for Christ, and Walter wanted so much to go there as a missionary. Well, he would just have to look for another door.

Soon he learned of an important Baptist church in the American Midwest that might be interested in calling a well-trained young minister like Rauschenbusch as their pastor. The pulpit committee listened to his preaching, studied his qualifications, and interviewed him. Surely, he felt, this church would call him to their pulpit. But nothing happened. Obviously, a second door had been closed. Walter could neither go to India as a missionary nor become the pastor of a fine city church.

What then? At last, to his surprise, a door did open—not a very pretty or promising door, but nevertheless a door. A little congregation, the Second German Baptist Church of New York City, composed mostly of poor people living in one of the city's worst slum neighborhoods, asked him to become their pastor. True to his belief in divine guidance, Walter reasoned that this must be where God wanted him; so he accepted the call to this unpromising ministry.

In this urban jungle known as Hell's Kitchen, Walter Rauschenbusch served for eleven years as pastor on a salary of $600 a year, ministering to life in the raw. Not only did he preach Christ and teach the Bible but also he served his people by grappling at firsthand with problems such as malnutrition, destitution, overcrowded tenements, unemployment, sickness without proper medical care, drunkenness, prostitution, the exploitation of the poor, and the crime-breeding streets of the slums. He worked for playgrounds and decent housing, and he fought with hot indignation against corruption in high places.

Inevitably Rauschenbusch gained profound insights into social problems through this ministry in the slums which led him to a second conversion. In his new experience of God's calling he gained a whole new outlook on the meaning of the gospel and the kingdom of God. His life became marked by an even greater social passion than he had previously known.

Church leaders criticized him severely. "It is not the mission of the church to abolish physical misery," they said. "It should concentrate on saving souls." But Rauschenbusch did not agree, and he doubted that they would ever really understand him. The social concern which motivated him so deeply had not come from the traditional, unfeeling, self-centered churches that had become his severest critics. "It came from the outside," he said. "It came through personal contact with poverty. When I saw how men toiled all their lifelong, hard, toilsome lives, and at the end had almost nothing to show for it, how strong men begged for work and could not get it; how little children died—oh! the children's funerals! They gripped my heart."

Studying the Bible more deeply, Rauschenbusch discovered a further insight. He reasoned that there was no conflict "between a gospel for the individual and a gospel big enough to redeem the whole social system." He came to believe that whereas "our inherited Christian faith dealt with individuals, our present task deals with society."

The fierce energies he expended in service to the poor so weakened his strength, however, that in 1888 he was stricken with a severe attack of the flu, which caused him to become deaf. For the last thirty years of his life, therefore, he lived with a sense of loneliness because he could not hear. Perhaps, however, this shutting out of human noise and distractions helped to quicken his spiritual perception and enabled him to think deeply and to write powerfully.

And then another door opened, the one for which everything in his life had been preparing him. In 1897 the Rochester Theological Seminary, his alma mater, called him to its campus to teach young people preparing for the ministry. There for twenty-one years his classroom became the center of his concern for the social interpretation of the gospel.

In awakening the complacent churches to the dire social problems of the day, Rauschenbusch often drew upon his own rugged experiences for illustrations. For example, in dealing with the problems of the laboring man in a society of wealth, he recalled those hot summer days when he had worked on the farm. Attacking the concentration of wealth in the hands of a few people, he wrote: "Wealth is to a nation what manure is to a farm. If the farmer spreads it evenly over the soil, it will enrich the whole. If he should leave it in heaps, the land would be impoverished and under the rich heaps the vegetation would be killed."

Dr. Rauschenbusch now began to put his ideas into books that commanded national attention. He pleaded that religion should take its proper and important part in solving the social crises of the times. He brought his biblical studies to bear upon the relation of social issues to the kingdom of God. His great book *Christianity and the Social Crisis,* published in 1907, hit the reading public just at the time when Americans were beginning to have an uneasy conscience about social problems. Christian leaders began to be upset by the injustice of sweatshops, the forced labor of children in factories, and the spread of disease in crowded slums. A breeze of social reform could be felt sweeping across the country, and his book intensified it to a powerful wind which blew away the church's complacency.

Books now began to flow from this social prophet's pen. *For God and the People: Prayers of the Social Awakening* appeared in 1910 and *Christianizing the Social Order* in 1912. His last great book, *A Theology for the Social Gospel,* was published in 1917, reflecting his long experience and mature thinking. Meanwhile he continued to play a conspicuous part in the American scene. By his lectures, writing, preaching, teaching, and counsel, he prodded the American conscience toward social reform.

The coming of World War I was a great tragedy for Rauschenbusch. Never a lover of war and always abhorring bloodshed, he wore crepe on his lapel to express his grief over the fighting. Many people misunderstood his motives because of his German name and ancestry and tormented him until his death from cancer in 1918, but he never wavered from his conviction. As he felt death approaching, he wrote to a friend: "Since 1914 the world is full of hate, and I cannot expect to be happy again in this lifetime." Near death, he said: "I am not sorry to be leaving a world where there is so much hate and to be going to a country where there will be so much love."

In a sense, he has never left this world. His ministry still goes on. Thousands of young people who studied under Walter Rauschenbusch carried his spirit forward in their lives as Christian ministers, and countless others who in turn heard their preaching and teaching continue his work to this day.

16

JOHN FROST

A Crow Indian Who Broke His Vow

On a hill overlooking the Crow Indian camp in the Bighorn Mountains of Wyoming, the woman named Strong Face stood alone with her little son Red Neck, her arms lifted in adoration to the Great Spirit who ruled the tribe. As she chanted a song of mourning, tears flowed down her face. It was the ancient religious ceremony of vengeance in which a small boy is consecrated to hatred. She prayed that he might become a warrior of courage and sure marksmanship in order that he might kill his enemies.

"Promise me," she urged, "that some day you will kill a Sioux that the death of your father may be avenged." And in response the boy made his vow, his arms extended upward as Strong Face invoked the sun's blessing upon him.

Red Neck was a Crow by adoption. His father had been a white settler on the frontier, his mother a Blackfoot Indian. In 1871, when Red Neck was only six months old, a group of Sioux warriors under Chief Sitting Bull had murdered his father in a raid upon the Blackfoot village, and Strong Face had been left to care for her little son alone. Now, however, they lived with the Crows, and the chief of this tribe had adopted Red Neck as his own son.

The boy learned the legends of both the Crow and the Blackfoot as he grew to maturity. With his mother he worshiped the spirits that according to the tribal religion resided in the sun, the lightning, the rivers, and the rocks. He became expert with the rifle as well as the bow and arrow, and he could track deer and bear successfully.

But the day of the plains Indian was passing. It was late in the nineteenth century, and white civilization was closing in. Recognizing the need for more than a tribal education, Red Neck enrolled in the government school at the Crow Agency in Montana. It was not easy for him to make the transition to modern ways. In the evenings he would ride off on his pony into the mountains to gaze wistfully at the distant hunting grounds of his people out on the prairie and think of returning to the old life. But deep down he knew that he would not go back.

Doing well in his studies, Red Neck was soon transferred to the famous Indian school in Pennsylvania known as Carlisle Institute, where he adopted his father's family name and became known as John Frost. Nevertheless, his Indian feelings still ran deep. They surfaced when the news came from Wounded Knee.

The story, like so many of those involving American Indians, is a tragic one. Gold had been discovered in South Dakota, which was Sioux country, and the coming of prospectors and other white people had led to clashes with the Indians. Famous chiefs, such as Big Foot, Kicking Bear, and Sitting Bull, committed to the defense of their tribal lands, had warred against the invading whites, and Sitting Bull had been killed in the final battle, at Wounded Knee.

The young Crow studying at Carlisle Institute, elated over the killing of the chief who had been responsible for his father's death, let out a yell of savage glee in the school library. Some of the other Indians, however, had different ideas, especially Big Horse, a nephew of Sitting Bull, who challenged Red Neck over this insult to his family. The Sioux and the Crow began to slug it out with their fists. Red Neck, the more skillful of the two, dropped Big Horse to the floor with a series of short jabs to the chin. As the Sioux, almost unconscious, crawled toward him, the enraged Red Neck seized a chair, preparing to fulfill his boyhood vow by killing his enemy.

Just then a voice called him back to reality: "Come to my office, John." As his senses returned, the young Indian told Captain Pratt of the solemn promise to avenge the death of his father, a promise which he had made to the sun in his mother's presence. "I knew your father," said the captain. "He was a good man, but the days of blood vengeance are over. Calm down, and we'll not discipline you for this."

John continued his studies at Carlisle. He became a captain in the military cadet corps and played on the school's first football team,

which was later to achieve national recognition. He learned some of the social amenities and began to study the Bible. Upon his graduation he was one of twenty who returned to the Crow reservation to work for the United States Government. There he served first as a dormitory counselor in the Crow Agency school and later as a scout and an interpreter at Fort Custer.

In time Frost came in touch with Baptist missionaries working among the Crows and was converted to Christ. He became active in the church and studied the Bible intently. In 1927 as a man in his fifties he was ordained to the Christian ministry and became pastor of the Baptist church at Pryor, Montana. He became a strong witness for Christ and a popular speaker.

Delivering an address at the Northern Baptist Convention in Chicago that same year, he recalled his childhood and the barbarous religious customs he had known among the Indians as they sought to appease the Great Spirit and the animals, birds, streams, and springs which were considered to be the Spirit's messengers.

"In order to gain favor from these many message carriers of the Great Spirit," he said, "worshipers would go to the mountains and choose some high point, then fast for days, neither eating nor drinking. In some cases they would chop off the index finger at the first joint as a sacrifice, or tear strips of skin from the body as an offering. . . . Thank God, these terrible things are not seen anymore. Great changes have taken place and many of the Crows are rejoicing in a Savior's love, and climbing the trail to that happy land above."

But Frost's greatest Christian testimony, the one which rounded out his life, was the renunciation of his boyhood vow, which occurred a few years later at the dedication of a chapel for Indians at Lodge Grass, Montana. This is what he said: "When I was a boy, I made a vow to the Great Spirit that I would have as my life-purpose avenging the death of my father who was murdered by the Sioux. For many, many years my heart was filled with hatred. Whenever I thought of the Sioux, the desire arose within me to fulfill my vow. But God had other plans for me."

A Congregational pastor from the Sioux tribe, named Iron Moccasin, stood next to him. John placed his arm about Iron Moccasin's shoulder and declared: "I thank God that I can call this Sioux my brother."

17

HELEN BARRETT MONTGOMERY

Forerunner of Today's Woman

The story of Helen Barrett Montgomery wouldn't seem very special if it had happened in the latter part of the twentieth century. By that time people had come to expect that women would occupy an important place in the life of the church and community and would be known for scholarly achievements.

But her great years were long before that. They came in the first quarter of the twentieth century, when the battle to establish women's right to vote was still going on—a time when women might work as housemaids, typists, nurses, or perhaps schoolteachers, but not at many other occupations. Woman's place was in the home, and if she was married, she stayed there caring for her husband and children. She certainly didn't take an active part in the big world outside.

Helen was different, though. Without feeling the need to be militant or assertive about it, she devotedly followed her conviction to serve humanity in whatever God required. In the process she became one of her country's great religious and civic leaders. And, for a woman in her day, that was a daring thing to do.

"Life seemed so grand and beautiful as we rose from our knees," she wrote to a friend in a burst of joy following her engagement to William A. Montgomery, a Philadelphia businessman. The part about the knees was especially significant, for Helen and William made their betrothal an act of prayer, given while both knelt in reverence before Almighty God. "I am anxious," continued the letter, "that my whole life may be given without reserve to God's service. . . . Before he [William] went away, he knelt with me and together we consecrated our lives to God's work in the world, promising to make this work our first thought."

And so they were married, but it would be oversimplification to say that they lived happily ever after.

In the early days of Helen and William's marriage, automobiles were not started just by turning a key. A crank handle hung from the front of the car just below the radiator, and the would-be driver had to rotate it vigorously by hand to turn the motor over and get it running. It was hard work, and sometimes the crank handle would swing back and strike the person's arm with enough force to break a bone. Helen was talking to William about just such an incident.

"William!" she called as she put the receiver of the old-fashioned telephone back on its hook. "Did you hear that John Cousins broke his wrist yesterday morning while trying to crank his car when it was so awfully cold?"

"No, but worse yet, the morning paper reports that Harold White forgot to put on the emergency brake before he began to crank his car; the engine started suddenly and his car ran over him. He's on the critical list at the hospital." Mr. Montgomery was greatly disturbed. "You know, my dear," he continued, "there is a young inventor who has a device that could correct this, if only he could perfect it and put it on the market. It is an electric self-starter that will do away with all these broken wrists and run-over bodies because people will be able to start their cars automatically from the driver's seat. I believe in this, and I'm going to back him financially."

As we know today, the idea was a good one. For considerably more than half a century, no automobile has been built without a starter. But to people of that time it was a foolish and impractical gadget. Mr. Montgomery poured money, then more money, and still more money into the new invention, but nobody wanted it. Soon he was on the edge of bankruptcy.

William and Helen believed in the self-starter, and Helen wanted to do her part in the family's financial crisis. At that time they lived in a beautiful home in Rochester, New York, where Helen's most prized possession was a magnificent concert grand piano—the kind which world-famous artists use when they perform in the great concert halls. Secretly, while her husband was away at the office, she sold it, and then she gave him the money. Their pastor at the Lake Avenue

Baptist Church, hearing of the great sacrifice she had made, realized that the once-wealthy Montgomerys were in serious financial trouble. Even so, they were still among the church's most generous contributors. Wishing to help, he called on the couple and urged them to reduce their church pledge to a small amount, but they refused. "That is the last economy we would practice," they said.

God saw them through this time of troubles. The invention became a success. Soon it was a *great* success. The automobile starter became widely used, and finally the crank disappeared entirely. The Montgomerys profited greatly from their investment in this important invention and became very wealthy. But they did not join the "idle rich." They dedicated their fortune to the service of God.

Now that Mr. and Mrs. Montgomery were once more in comfortable circumstances, Helen resumed her studies of Greek, which she had begun as a student at Wellesley College. She was an excellent Greek student and loved the language for its beauty. Soon her knowledge of this ancient language was put to an important use. The American Baptist Publication Society, to mark the first hundred years of its history, wanted to publish a significant book which would exemplify one of its chief objectives, that of circulating the Scriptures. For this purpose Helen Barrett Montgomery translated into English, out of the original Greek, the entire New Testament. It was just the book the Society was seeking, and was published as the Centenary Translation.

No woman had ever done this before. It was still considered presumptuous for anybody to do a new translation of Bible texts. Was not the King James Version good enough? Or, if one must be modern, the revision known as the American Standard Version? A whole new translation? And by a woman, of all people? Unthinkable! But the Montgomery translation was well received. While her work was scholarly, it was also done in the words of everyday life, carrying out the spirit of its writers, who also had used the language of the people in *their* times. It met with instant acclaim and has continued to be so popular that it has been reprinted dozens of times and is still published under the title *The New Testament in Modern English*.

Helen Barrett Montgomery was deeply interested not only in the Bible but in missions as well. For ten years she served with great distinction as president of the Woman's American Baptist Foreign

Mission Society. In this office her influence reached beyond her own Baptist fellowship as she stirred Christian women of many denominations to help found and support seven colleges for the women of Asia.

In 1921 American Baptists conferred the highest possible honor upon her by electing her president of what was then called the Northern Baptist Convention, later the American Baptist Churches in the U.S.A., and she presided over the great annual convention the following year in Indianapolis. Not only was she the first woman to hold this high office, but also it was a quarter of a century before another of her sex held the same position.

In her home city of Rochester she became an outstanding civic leader, working vigorously for expanded educational opportunities for women and for the right of educated women to have a place of influence in the community. She organized discussion groups to sharpen the moral and ethical awareness of women and campaigned for civic reform. She chaired a committee to raise funds for opening the University of Rochester to women, and this goal was accomplished. She was the first woman to serve on the school board of her city and during her ten years of service played a leading part in improving the quality of education and taking the school system out of politics.

Helen Montgomery received many honorary degrees in her lifetime, and upon her death left nearly half a million dollars to hospitals, colleges, missions, and other Christian causes.

Unlike many heroic Baptists who dared, Helen Montgomery was never persecuted, never went to jail, never braved the perils of a strange and untamed land. Her daring was of a different sort. Great person that she was, as gracious and feminine as any you could find anywhere, nevertheless she never let her sex prevent her from doing whatever she believed God intended for her. She was a pioneer among Baptist women, one of the loveliest who ever lived. Her influence still goes on in the lives of those who are touched by institutions she founded and supported and by the living words of her Scripture translation which thousands of people still read.

18

JENNIE CLARE ADAMS

Poet Laureate of the Hopevale Martyrs

Living in a lonely forest
War clouds darkening the earth,
Stripped of treasures I had valued,
Things that once had seemed of worth. . . .

Jennie Adams paused to look at the words she had written. Writing poetry was a way of understanding her feelings and communicating them to others, as despair and hope, doom and opportunity swirled through her mind and heart. It had been more than a year since that day in December, 1941, when World War II had hit the Philippines. The United States Army had evacuated the Baptist mission hospital from the coastal city of Capiz on the island of Panay, where she had served as the superintendent of nurses for almost twenty years. The staff had tried to continue their work at a temporary inland location, but even this had proved impossible as news of the advancing Japanese forces reached them.

Now the little group of eleven missionary doctors, nurses, and wives, with the seven-year-old son of one of the couples, had escaped to a small clearing in an evergreen forest near the top of a mountain, reached only by a winding and difficult trail. Hiding under banana trees from time to time to avoid being seen from enemy planes that circled overhead, they had built huts of grass and palm leaves fastened to timbers cut from the forest, and floored with gravel or split bamboo. "We are now safe," one of the missionaries wrote in a letter that was smuggled to America, but "safety in the ordinary sense is a relative matter in Panay," for the danger was always present that they would be discovered by scouts from the forest or sky and taken prisoners.

The refugee missionaries lived like the people in the area, eating well but using much ingenuity to put meals together. They made flour from green bananas, rice, or corn; vinegar from wild bananas or pineapple parings, coffee from roasted corn and peanuts, and tea from ginger root. The villagers were good to them, bringing hundreds of eggs each week, and sometimes pork, beef, or chicken.

Within this primitive little village which they called "Hopevale" was a special place that they treasured above all others, a chapel in a beautiful, deep, dry gorge, where they had constructed seats, an altar, a pulpit, and a lectern of rocks and wood. There they worshiped every Sunday except when the Japanese were known to be nearby. With this woodland chapel as their base, the missionaries continued their ministry of preaching, teaching, and healing among the Philippine people. Constantly the roar of planes and distant gunfire and the rumors of prowling military parties reminded them of their peril.

Jennie must have written many of her poems while meditating in the chapel, but she was in her kitchen when she composed the lines with which this tale began. This small, gentle, soft-spoken Nebraskan in her middle forties was writing the poem as a birthday gift to another of the missionaries, her good friend Louise Rounds, wife of a preacher and mother of seven-year-old Erle, the child in the group. The title of the poem was "Orchids," and in it Jennie wanted to convey some of the beauty of these gorgeous purple, pink, and white blossoms which grew wild, high in the trees, and which she often collected to beautify her hut.

She continued to write:

> Though I'm barefoot in the kitchen
> With its dirt and gravel floor,
> I'm not poor while I have orchids
> Blooming at my kitchen door. . . .
>
> Pure and sweet they never fail me;
> Though the days may seem more drear,
> When I look into their faces
> I can find a bit of cheer.
> Unmolested by the war clouds

Or the cannon's distant boom,
Unperturbed they still continue
On their mossy boughs to bloom.

Jennie's life on Panay before the war, like that of the other missionaries, had been one of loyal and brave service to Christ. As head nurse at the Emmanuel Hospital she had taught a Bible class for the young Philippine girls in training. She had made long journeys on foot, often walking through mud and risking attack by the dangerous water buffalo, to visit villages where no white woman had ever gone before. There she had ministered to their aches and pains, their tropical ulcers and sicknesses, and had told them about Jesus, the Great Physician. One of the villages was Panitan, noted for its depravity, cock fights, and squalor, a place whose very name is translated "to take the skin off." There, at a considerable risk to her safety, she told Bible stories to the children against the opposition of their parents, and eventually she built a church that was later destroyed by a typhoon and rebuilt.

Hopevale was different, though. There was only tedious waiting and praying and struggling to exist, while performing what little ministry was possible with no resources and few people. But for Jennie there were the poems she wrote for herself and for others. In March, 1943, she wrote the one which most fully expresses her faith and that of the other refugees at Hopevale, a poem which perhaps some musician will someday set to music and thus create a great Christian hymn:

Let me live bravely;
For life has many battle fields
Where valor must be shown,
Many darkened corners,
Where pain and fear are known.
Life calls for sacrifice,
To share the highest good,
To serve courageously,
Sometimes to give life's blood.
As others lived and gave,
Let me be brave.

Let me serve faithfully;
Content with work to do,
Whatever life may bring,

In serving others well,
Thus do I serve my King.
May I not weary grow,
When tasks seem burdensome,
Nor turn aside distraught,
Before life's work is done.
    As others served—proved true,
    Let me be faithful too.

Let me witness clearly,
That be my sacred call,
In Christ to live and move,
For Him to give my all.
To Him all glory be,
My glory but His cross;
Except to live for Him,
I count my life but loss.
    As others witness clear and true,
    So may I witness too.

Let me die heroically,
Steadfast in faith and calm,
When that great day is near,
Knowing no hour of dread,
Feeling no anxious fear;
For death is but a door,
Closed tight on pain and strife,
A door that opens up
That we may enter life.
    As heroes die still brave and true
    Let me die too.

The death which Jennie foresaw in the final stanza arrived before the year was out. Almost two years had passed since the outbreak of war. The secret of Hopevale was becoming more difficult to keep as time passed. The Filipinos who came to study and worship with the missionaries had heard that word was out. The Japanese military knew of the little settlement, though they were not sure of its location. They were searching the mountains systematically, and it was probably just a matter of time before they would arrive. Finally, on December 19, the dreaded moment came. A party of soldiers discovered Hopevale and captured its residents. The next day, they put the entire group of missionaries to death, including the little boy.

The names of the Hopevale martyrs, like those of ancient time to whom the Book of Revelation is dedicated, are "written in the Book of Life":

> Jennie Clare Adams
> James and Charma Covell
> Dorothy Antoinette Dowell
> Signe Amelia Erickson
> Frederick and Ruth Meyer
> Francis and Gertrude Rose
> Erle and Louise Rounds and their son Erle

We know what happened in those two years at Hopevale through a few letters from some of the missionaries to American friends, smuggled out by Philippine Baptists, and also through some later reports by Philippine people, but most of all by the poems of Jennie Adams. It was her friend Ruth Meyer, also a martyr, who preserved them by sending copies to Philippine friends in one of the villages, and they in turn passed them along to Rebecca Rio, an instructor at Central Philippine College. To protect them from being confiscated, because almost anything written in English was suspicious, Miss Rio sewed them in a pillow just as Ann Judson had protected her husband's Burmese New Testament translation a century earlier. After the war she sent them to America.

Of all the poems in the pillow, the one Rebecca Rio liked best was one which Jennie Adams, contrasting her childhood home on the Nebraska prairies against her present refuge in the mountains of Panay, had titled "The Hills Shall Not Imprison Me." Responding to this, Rebecca wrote one of her own entitled "The Hills Did Not Imprison Her," dedicated to Jennie, which concludes with these lines:

> She did not let those hills imprison her;
> When sudden threat brought flight and fear,
> She knew that soon a day of victory
> Would break the bonds of war and set her free. . . .
>
> The day did come, more glorious than her dream,
> For the trail Home was paved with golden gleam,
> The Father's Greater Prairie Land where she
> Could say, "Those hills did not imprison me."

Baptists have expressed their love and appreciation for the

sacrifice of the Hopevale martyrs by constructing a replica of the historic woodland chapel. Located at the assembly grounds at Green Lake, Wisconsin, it is known as the Cathedral in the Glen.* To reach it, you must walk a wooded trail which recaptures the spirit of Hopevale not only by its shady quietness but also by some of Jennie Adams's poems which you pause to read as you approach the place of worship. Finally you sit on a log, quietly contemplating a rustic cross on a pile of rocks as she must have done in her own wooded sanctuary on the island of Panay when she wrote:

> Cathedral in the woodland, sheltering resting place,
> Where one may meditate and seek the Father's face;
> Cathedral in the woodland, shaded, calm, and still,
> In quietude we wait to know the Father's will.

In that spot, remembering those who gave their lives for Christ at Hopevale, you bow your head in silent prayer.

---

*The Cathedral in the Glen also memorializes Robert L. Moore, Jr., a young Baptist airman who lost his life while stationed in Manila during World War II.

19

THOMASINE ALLEN

Where the Need Was Greatest

A vibrant, white-haired American woman stood on the platform of the school auditorium in Kuji, Japan, on a summer day in 1958, surrounded by officials of the church and government. The room grew quiet as the Governor of the Prefecture lifted a jeweled decoration from a small, black lacquerware box and, holding a scroll, read the Emperor's message conferring upon her the Fifth Order of Merit of the Sacred Jewel. The woman was Thomasine Allen, an American Baptist missionary who had been the Emperor's prisoner during World War II in the internment camps of Sendai and Tokyo from 1941 to 1943. Now she was receiving one of the highest honors the Emperor could bestow. How did this come about?

Tommy (as she was called by her American friends) had grown up in Franklin, Indiana, among the students and faculty of nearby Baptist-related Franklin College where she herself became a student. There, caught up in the missionary enthusiasm of a group known as the Student Volunteer Movement, she dedicated her life to serving Christ in overseas missions. Upon application to the Woman's American Baptist Foreign Mission Society, recently formed under the leadership of Helen Barrett Montgomery, she was accepted at the age of twenty-five and assigned to work in Japan.

When Tommy arrived in Tokyo in 1915, Japan was very different from the great industrial nation of today. Though business and industry were thriving and Japan was becoming recognized as a world power, only fifty years had passed since the young Meiji Emperor Mutsohito had put an end to two and one-half centuries of total isolation from the rest of the world and had begun the process of modernizing the country. Many of the old customs and characteristics remained, especially outside the major cities.

In Tommy's first assignment, as principal of the Sarah Curtis Home, a girls' school in the great metropolis of Tokyo, she made her acquaintance with Japanese life, language, and customs. Then, ready for a more truly Japanese environment, she was transferred to Shokei Jo Gakuin, a girls' school in Sendai, a smaller city some two hundred miles north along the coast. Life there was pleasant as she taught the gentle, obedient Japanese girls and enjoyed the parties and the flowers.

Many women would have welcomed the opportunity to spend a lifetime in Sendai, but not Tommy. She knew there was a rural Japan out beyond that wasn't gentle or pleasant or easy, a Japan where the need for Christian mission was much greater than in a refined girls' school, and she determined to find it. First she went back to America to strengthen her educational background with a master's degree at the University of Chicago. Then, returning to Japan in 1929 with a new assignment, she began work in Morioka, an inland city on the frontier where Western culture and the Christian faith were little known.

In Morioka Tommy had to learn a new kind of living. She cooked with Japanese charcoal fire pots in a dark and dirty kitchen which required much scrubbing. She tried unsuccessfully to keep herself warm in a house which basically was no more than a light framework fitted with sliding doors and shutters for walls, rice straw matting *(tatami)* on the floors, and inadequate wood stoves for heat. Her work, too, was more demanding than previously, for she now supervised a kindergarten, directed women's and children's work in struggling Baptist churches of the area, and managed a community center on the edge of town near the rice paddies. Her work reached out into the outlying areas, including such places as Matsuo Kozan, a mining town reached only by a two-hour walk on mountain trails from the end of the railroad line.

But even Morioka was not enough of a challenge to satisfy Tommy. As she became increasingly aware of the poverty and hardship of Japanese rural life, she felt the call to push on from the cities to the frontier. "I want to go where the need is greatest," she said. That place had to be Kuji, still farther north, and Tommy applied successfully for permission to transfer there, a community of farmers, fishermen, and miners "at the end of the line."

Tommy's home in Kuji when she arrived in 1938 was known in the neighborhood as the haunted house, but the ghost gave her no problems. Of greater concern was the hard physical labor needed to make the place livable—the scrubbing of floors and walls, the opening of clogged drains, the cutting of weeds, the hauling of water from the town pump. The only bathtub available was a big wooden one which wouldn't fit in the house; so she used it outdoors with some of the women holding up quilts to protect her privacy. Not so good in winter!

There was a kindergarten which Takeshi Yahaba, one of the Japanese workers, described as terribly dark and dirty. "We had no toys or playthings," he recalled, "only a swing made of a piece of rope hung from the limb of a tree. We had no chairs either, but we were able to pick up some tangerine crates and we brought them to use as stools. We did have snakes in the yard, but we finally killed most of them. Worse than anything, though, was having to use this terribly dark, unsanitary room for the children."

With great difficulty Tommy and Mr. Yahaba arranged to buy an acre of land to construct a new kindergarten. It was an odd-shaped, barren plot but the only one available. As construction was about to begin, however, Tommy was summoned to the police office and informed that she would have to sell it to a railroad which was building a spur track to the mines. Tommy and Mr. Yahaba pleaded with the chief for three hours, stressing the spiritual values taught in a Christian school, until finally the chief relented. "You may keep your land as far as the police are concerned," he said. "We can't do anything with people who have the faith that you have." In spite of this action, surveyors for the railroad came to prepare for construction of the track, but repeatedly Mr. Yahaba and Tommy declared, "We are not going to give it up," and finally the surveyors went away.

The railroad problem, however, was only the beginning of the troubles of putting up a building in Kuji. Carpenters walked off the job because they didn't understand the Western type of construction Tommy wanted. The government's Architecture Department created problems with red tape. There were shortages of most materials, especially nails. Tommy and her co-workers collected old nails and straightened them, but the problem was not solved until she went to China and bought twenty kegs of nails.

Finally the project was completed, and it proved to be worth all the effort it had required. The bright, clean, airy building attracted far more children than it could accommodate, and soon an excellent kindergarten was in full operation. Furthermore, people of the community, seeing the advantages of a clean, well-built structure, began to repair and improve their own properties.

But bad trouble was on the way. It was obvious to many that tensions were building up between Japan and the United States. The State Department advised the missionaries to go home, but Tommy stubbornly remained in Kuji. She sensed that as an American she was being shadowed by the police, and yet she encountered no real hostility because her work in the community was so deeply appreciated. Finally, on December 7, 1941, the Japanese attacked Pearl Harbor, and on that same morning five policemen came to arrest her.

What followed was a two-year internment for Tommy along with other missionaries, not only Baptists but also those of many Protestant and Catholic groups. Internment during wartime is a common procedure, and in World War II both Japan and the United States practiced it. It is not quite the same as imprisonment, for the internee is not placed in a cell but is restricted to a very limited location and not allowed to travel. The United States interned in concentration camps thousands of Japanese citizens living in this country, as well as a great many United States citizens of Japanese ancestry. One of the latter was Jitsuo Morikawa, who attained renown after the war as a Baptist pastor and evangelist.

During the first few months in which Tommy and the other Americans were interned in Japan, they were held under house arrest at the home of a missionary in Morioka under the constant threat of imprisonment. Then for six months Tommy and another American Baptist woman, Alice Bixby, were interned at Sendai. Following this Tommy was moved to a large concentration camp in Tokyo, where she found many old friends, including Dr. and Mrs. William Axling, who are remembered among the great missionary leaders in Japan.

Conditions in the camp were crowded and food was scarce; the women had to do much hard work but were not mistreated. Finally, late in 1943, they returned to the United States through an exchange of prisoners.

Returning to Kuji after the war, Tommy found that the mission had been kept alive through the efforts of Mr. Yahaba and other Japanese people. Conditions in general were very bad, though, as a result of the bombings and the tremendous cost of the war. There was nothing to buy in the stores, and everyone was hungry. Many people were living in shacks built from salvaged wood, packing boxes, and battered tin on land that had been cleared of rubble and ashes. But things slowly improved.

The work of the mission prospered in the postwar years. The people remembered that Tommy had not left them in the dangerous months just before the outbreak of war but had risked and actually experienced internship by staying at her post. Appreciating this loyalty, they responded warmly now to her leadership, and the Center grew and prospered. Baptismal services were held for fifteen persons in September and fourteen more in December. A Baptist church was organized, which, through evangelism, soon extended its influence to a nearby town. Some of the people studied and introduced new and improved farming methods. As time went on, the growing church sponsored Sunday schools and evangelistic meetings in not just one but many nearby towns and villages. A hospital was built. An elementary school was added to the kindergarten. A demonstration farm and an agricultural school were opened to teach the farmers how to make better use of their land.

In later years Kuji's Japanese Christians themselves provided more and more leadership in the development of their city as a healthy, vital community where Christ is known by all and loved by many, but behind it all was the guiding, inspiring spirit of Thomasine Allen, a Baptist woman who went "where the need was greatest." Do you wonder that His Majesty the Emperor of Japan would think her worthy of one of his most honored medals?

20

MARTIN LUTHER KING, JR.

Preacher with a Dream

"It's time for action, Coretta," said the young pastor of the Dexter Avenue Baptist Church to his wife. "Our people have put up with this abuse long enough!"

Coretta was not surprised. She understood the deep Christian commitment and intense social concern of the man she had married only two years earlier. "Yes, Martin," she replied. "What happened to Rosa Parks here in Montgomery, Alabama, is just one more thing in the long line of insults that we black people have suffered through the years, but people are near the breaking point. What do you propose to do?"

Martin Luther King, Jr., sat for a few moments in silence, remembering the Rosa Parks' incident. It really wasn't anything spectacular in itself, but it had caught people's imagination. Rosa was a black working woman who was very tired after a long day on the job. She had boarded a bus to ride home, and because the back seats customarily assigned to people of her race were taken, she had selected an unoccupied place near the center of the bus. This was all right until a white man boarded the bus and, finding the seats reserved for whites in the front section occupied, demanded that she get up and let him sit in her place. Mrs. Parks, bone-weary from her day's work, refused to yield. The bus driver demanded that she release her seat to the white man. Again she refused. The bus driver called a policeman, and she was arrested.

Martin remembered that there had been other incidents like this in Montgomery during the two years he had lived there. One particularly stuck in his mind. A fifteen-year-old girl had been handcuffed and jailed for refusing to give up her place to a white passenger. Other black persons had been arrested for the same offense, and one black man had been shot to death for refusing to yield his seat. The traditional and insulting rule that "blacks ride in the back" had become unbearable.

Just then the telephone rang. It was E. D. Nixon, a friend of Rosa Parks. "Dr. King," said the voice on the telephone, "we must do something about this insult to Mrs. Parks. I've been talking with the Reverend Ralph Abernathy of First Baptist Church, and he agrees that all black people should refuse to ride the city buses all day this coming Monday. Would you help us to organize the boycott?"

With that historic telephone call on the morning of December 2, 1955, Martin Luther King, Jr., was launched upon a historic crusade which was to shake the entire nation.

The bus boycott in Montgomery was successfully organized and carried out by the newly formed Montgomery Improvement Association, with King as its president. The buses, carrying white passengers only that Monday, had light loads as the black people used car pools, bicycles, or shoe leather to reach their destinations. In the evening the leaders met to talk it over. "We must continue the boycott," they declared, "until black passengers are treated decently and black bus drivers are hired for routes in our own neighborhoods." They did not demand completely open seating on the buses—only that seats should be available on a first-come, first-served basis, with whites starting from the front and blacks from the back.

Some of those present argued for more violent measures against the bus company, but King opposed such action. As a student he had been deeply interested in the nonviolent protests of the great Mohandas K. Gandhi which had overcome many of the injustices existing in India, and King believed in Gandhi's way. He told the meeting: "Our actions must be guided by the deepest principles of our Christian faith. . . . Once again we must hear the words of Jesus echoing across the centuries: 'Love your enemies, bless them that curse you, and pray for them that despitefully use you.' If we fail to do this, our protest will end up as a meaningless drama on the stage of history, and its memory will be shrouded with the ugly garments of shame."

The bus boycott went on for more than a year. The Kings' home was bombed. Car-pool drivers were arrested and jailed for minor traffic offenses that under other circumstances might have been overlooked. Some lost their operators' licenses or had trouble getting their insurance renewed. More than a hundred leaders of the boycott, including King, were arrested and charged with conspiracy. King himself was sentenced to 386 days in jail but was released on bond when he appealed. The bus company, without its black passengers, tottered toward bankruptcy. Business activity in the city slowed to a crawl. Court battles raged.

Finally, by order of the United States Supreme Court, the bus company was obliged to abolish its policy of segregated seating, and on the morning of December 22, 1956, young Pastor King became the first black person in the history of Montgomery, Alabama, to board a city bus and take a seat of his choosing.

This incident, of course, was only the beginning of King's campaign for civil rights, and no story as brief as this could cover it all. There were many high points, however, which made their mark on history. Through all of these he insisted on the principle of nonviolence as a true expression of the Christian ideal. The Ebenezer Baptist Church in Atlanta, to which he went to share a great ministry with his illustrious father, became one of the great centers of the movement.

With King as their spiritual leader, thousands of young people, especially college students, both black and white, joined in a program known as Sit-ins. They would go to a lunch counter or restaurant or other public facility which had been barred to black people and insist upon service. Though punched, beaten, kicked, burned with cigarettes, arrested, and jailed, they refused to strike back physically but continued again and again to renew the sit-ins until eventually they would win and thus another establishment would accept black customers on an equal basis with whites. King himself was arrested while sitting in with a group of students at the restaurant in Rich's posh department store in downtown Atlanta and was sentenced to four months at hard labor. He was released through the efforts of presidential candidate John F. Kennedy and his brother Robert, both of whom, like King, were eventually to become martyrs.

Another nonviolent technique adopted by black people in this

107

period of time was Freedom Rides. They would buy tickets for trips on interstate bus lines in the South so as to challenge the segregated waiting rooms, toilets, and lunch counters at the bus stations by using these facilities which had been closed to blacks. As a result white resisters mobbed some of the buses. Tires were slashed; buses were burned; and black passengers were beaten by angry whites. Though King did not personally participate in the Freedom Rides, he encouraged them by speaking publicly in their support.

In Albany, Georgia, police drove a group of black students away from a bus terminal lunch counter and jailed them. A few days later they arrested more than four hundred black high school and college students marching on city hall in protest. Into this city burning with racial unrest Dr. King came to organize a Freedom March. He and the marchers were arrested, then released, and within a few months the city's resistance was as bitter as ever. King returned to Albany many times to rally support for nonviolent resistance and spent additional days in jail there.

In Birmingham, Alabama, church leaders asked Dr. King for his help in the battle for civil rights, including the removal of "White Only" and "Negro Only" signs from water fountains and rest rooms. King set out on a speaking tour which included twenty-eight speeches in sixteen cities to raise money and enlist volunteers for a civil rights campaign in Birmingham. Picketing and sit-ins by blacks began, and many were arrested, including Dr. King, who was placed in solitary confinement. There he wrote a statement known as "Letter from Birmingham Jail," which has become a classic. In it he charged that the denial of rights to black people, even when done under civil law, was a violation of the laws of God. Therefore, he promised, black people would continue to respect the higher laws of God by opposing unjust laws having only human authority. Eventually the power structures of Birmingham granted the blacks' demands.

The followers of Dr. King increased in numbers and enthusiasm as audiences of 10,000, 25,000, and even more gathered to hear him speak. In Detroit 125,000 joined in a Freedom Walk and became his audience for a stirring address. In 1963 he organized the March on Washington, and 200,000 people gathered before the steps of the Lincoln Memorial as he delivered his great speech, "I Have a Dream." Stirringly he told this throng and a huge TV audience as well

about his vision for a day in which his own children, and all Americans, would live in peace and equality with each other regardless of race or color. In his stirring conclusion, he declared: "When we let freedom ring, when we let it ring from every village and every hamlet, from every state and every city, we will be able to speed up that day when all God's children, black men and white men, Jews and Gentiles, Protestants and Catholics, will be able to join hands and sing in the words of that old Negro spiritual, 'Free at last! Free at last! Thank God almighty, we are free at last!'"

Partly as a result of this great march and the address which Dr. King delivered, the United States Congress was stirred to pass the Civil Rights Act of 1964, by which many of the reforms for which he had labored became the law of the land. During the same year in Oslo, Norway, he received the greatest honor of his lifetime, the Nobel Peace Prize. Yet just a few months later he was in jail again, this time for leading a march of a thousand black persons to the courthouse at Selma, Alabama, in connection with a campaign to register black voters.

What a tragedy it was for all Americans when this eminent Baptist leader was shot to death by an assassin in Memphis in April, 1968, where he had come to assist the city's garbage workers in their struggle for higher wages. There have been many strong personalities among the black people in their widespread movement for equality and recognition during the past half of the twentieth century, but none with so great a popular following, so strong a commitment to nonviolence, and so deep a love for Jesus Christ as Martin Luther King, Jr.

BIBLIOGRAPHY

Adams, Jennie Clare, *The Hills Did Not Imprison Her*. New York: Woman's American Baptist Foreign Mission Society, 1947.

Backus, Isaac, *History of the Baptists in New England*. Philadelphia: American Baptist Publication Society, 1844. (First published by Backus in 1777.)

Bicknell, Thomas W., *The Story of Dr. John Clarke*. Providence: Published by the author, 1915.

Brisbane, Robert H., *Black Activism*. Valley Forge: Judson Press, 1974.

Brittain, Vera, *Valiant Pilgrim, The Story of John Bunyan and Puritan England*. New York: Macmillan, Inc., 1950.

Browne, Benjamin P., *Tales of Baptist Daring*. Valley Forge: Judson Press, 1961.

Carey, Samuel Pearce, *William Carey*. London: Carey Press, 1934.

Cooke, John Hunt, *Johann Gerhard Oncken: His Life and Work*. London: S. W. Partridge and Co., 1908.

deBlois, Austen Kennedy, *Fighters for Freedom*. Valley Forge: Judson Press, 1929.

Fitts, Leroy, *Lott Carey: First Black Missionary to Africa*. Valley Forge: Judson Press, 1978.

Hemphill, Elizabeth Anne, *A Treasure to Share*. Valley Forge: Judson Press, 1964.

Hill, William A., ed., *The Moccasin Trail*. Valley Forge: Judson Press, 1932.

Hines, Herbert Waldo, *Clough: Kingdom-Builder in South India*. Valley Forge: Judson Press, 1929.

Judson, Edward, *The Life of Adoniram Judson.* New York: Anson D. F. Randolph & Co., 1883.

Landis, Benson Y., *A Rauschenbusch Reader.* New York: Harper & Row, Publishers, 1957.

Mays, Benjamin E., comp., *A Gospel for the Social Awakening: Writings of Walter Rauschenbusch.* New York: Association Press, 1950.

Montgomery, Helen Barrett, *Helen Barrett Montgomery.* Old Tappan, N.J.: Fleming H. Revell Company, 1940.

Montgomery, Helen Barrett, *The New Testament in Modern English.* Valley Forge: Judson Press, 1968.

Morrison, J. H., *William Carey, Cobbler and Pioneer.* London: Hodder and Stoughton, 1920.

Nelson, Wilbur, *The Hero of Aquidneck.* Old Tappan, N.J.: Fleming H. Revell Company, 1938.

Newman, A. H., *A History of the Baptists in the United States.* New York: Christian Literature Co., 1894.

Rogers, Truett, *Bibles and Battle Drums.* Valley Forge: Judson Press, 1976.

Sharpe, Dores Robinson, *Walter Rauschenbusch.* New York: Macmillan, Inc., 1942.

Stewart, Walter Sinclair, *Later Baptist Missionaries and Pioneers.* Valley Forge: Judson Press, 1928.

Torbet, Robert G., *A History of the Baptists.* rev. ed. Valley Forge: Judson Press, 1973.

Tull, James E., *Shapers of Baptist Thought.* Valley Forge: Judson Press, 1972.

Wilson, Jesse R., *Through Shining Archway.* New York: American Baptist Foreign Mission Society, 1945.

Woodson, Carter G., *The History of the Negro Church.* Washington: The Associated Publishers, 1972.